Your Success Starts Now

Timeless Principles to Help You Reach
Your Goals Faster & Accelerate
Your Path To Success

Your Success Starts Now

Timeless Principles to Help You Reach
Your Goals Faster & Accelerate
Your Path To Success

Published by: Strategies for Empowered Living Inc

Table of Contents

Introduction

Your Success Starts Now is a book of timeless principles designed to help you accelerate your path to success – your vision of your best life. In the pages ahead, you'll discover practical tips to help you reach your goals faster and overcome any internal roadblocks that are hindering your success. *Your Success Starts Now* is an important book to read if you desire to be successful because far too many people put their goals on hold and settle for a life of stagnation, rather than living out their vision. ...And you don't want to be that person! Far too many people settle for a life of mediocrity when there's greatness inside each and every one of us. Too many people die without ever fully utilizing their gifts and greatness. Don't let this be you!!!

Your success starts now. Not when the kids get older, or you lose the extra weight, not when you meet your Mr. or Mrs. Right, get out of debt or whatever other convenient excuses you've told yourself to justify coasting through life. The time to start living the life you desire is now. You can start living your best life now by taking small, incremental steps toward your goals and dreams, even if you don't have all the pieces in place just yet. Stop waiting for things to be perfect. Sometimes you have to take the leap when you're "ready enough" by progressively moving your life in the direction of your ultimate goals.

My success includes having my own business since 2000, being an award-winning author who has written and published more than ten highly-successful books that are widely utilized in the health and human service sector, youth organizations and churches. I am a respected leader in my industry, a consultant to several nonprofits, a highly-sought after speaker, and a former radio personality with Carib World Radio. I am the founder of Cassandra Mack Ministries, a Bible-centered teaching ministry that utilizes social media, live events, group challenges and a weekly Church By Phone service to share the message of the kingdom globally. And I am also a busy mom so I know what it's like to have multiple demands competing for your time and energy.

Like everyone else I've had challenges to overcome and personal setbacks. So, it's not about where you start out in life or what happens to you that defines how far you go on life. Ultimately, what matters most is that you choose to live each day with a sense of focus, personal power and purpose.

Success is not something that randomly happens to you. Success is a momentum that you create by the choices you make, the daily disciplines that you put into practice and the sustained effort that you put into your goals and dreams. So, whether you want to improve your lot in life, reinvent yourself, grow professionally, achieve a goal that requires you to stretch yourself, make a stronger impact in your industry or pursue your dreams with renewed determination, *Your Success Starts Now* will provide you with a set of principles to get from where you are now to where you want to be. Also included are selected Bible scriptures that you can reflect on to give you wisdom and spiritual strength for your journey.

See you on the path,

Cassandra Mack

Principle #1.
Believe That You Were Built To Win

If you truly want to live the life that you desire, the first step is to believe that it is possible for you to do so. No matter where you are in life, whether you are right where you want to be or you feel like you're falling behind, if you want to achieve your goals, you must believe that you have what it takes to do so.

Unfortunately, many people hold themselves back from living their most authentically fulfilling lives because they don't believe in themselves. And whatever we believe about ourselves at the deepest level usually becomes true for us. Why? Because, if we don't believe that it's possible to have the life we want, we won't even try to pursue our dreams.

When you fail to believe in yourself, you set yourself up for failure. The ironic thing about how the mind works is you won't even be aware that you are sabotaging your own success because when you operate from a place of self-doubt you tend not to think about how your own beliefs affect your actions. For example, let's say that you are considering starting a business, but in the back of your mind you don't believe that you can successfully pull it off, because of this discouraging self-doubt, you'll talk yourself out of your good ideas idea before you ever get them off the ground. If this is you, you've got to stop sabotaging your success by renewing your mind with beliefs that affirm your potential & capacity.

See the reality of life is this: When you choose to believe in yourself and act on your affirming beliefs with positive, persistent conviction you position yourself to win because you take a chance on you. Your own attitude of self-assurance will inspire you to step out of your comfort zone, press past the doubts and strive towards your goals. By believing in yourself, you reprogram your mind to direct all of your thoughts and actions toward the goals you want to achieve and the plans that you desire to accomplish.

Study after study in the area of personal achievement shows that the number one determining factor in your success is you - your belief in yourself and your daily disciplines towards creating the life you want. Therefore, if you do not believe in yourself – I'm talking about wholeheartedly believing in yourself, then your own self-doubt and insecurity will hold you back. But it doesn't have to be this way.

You can decide right now that you are going to choose to believe in yourself. You are already equipped with everything you need to succeed. You were not designed for stagnation. You were built to flourish & thrive. You have seeds of greatness inside of you, but it's up to you to cultivate your greatness. You may not be where you want to be right now. Perhaps you even have lots of obstacles to overcome or a few issues to work through, but this doesn't negate the fact that you have greatness inside of you.

So, the question for you is: What are you going to do with your greatness? Will you let you cultivate your gifts and commit yourself to learning new things or will you succumb to self-doubt? You get to decide!!!

What's important for you to know is that there are millions of people, some with more resources and many others with a lot less who are living their dreams, achieving their goals and creating fulfilling lives. So, if other people are living their desired lives, then it is certainly possible for you too.

Success starts in the mind. It starts with your beliefs and your internal narrative then extends to your choices and habits. Whether you call it confidence, self-esteem or the power of positive thinking, it all comes down to believing that you have what it takes to not only make it, but to live out your own personal vision of success. It's also knowing that whatever you don't have you can borrow, barter, outsource or learn. Believe that you were built to win.

Questions for You To Give Some Thought To

Following are some questions designed to get you thinking about ways to develop winning beliefs about yourself.

- Do you believe that you were built to win?
- What's your definition of a winner? How would you define a winning life? What about a winning attitude? Based on your definition of a winning attitude, do you possess one? If

11

not, what changes can you make right now to develop a more winning attitude?

- What winning qualities do you already posses? Name at least three. How can you use these qualities to accelerate your success so that you can get the results that you're striving for?

Action Steps

✓ Make a list of 3 things that you are proud of in your life and 3 things that you are grateful for. Keep this list handy to help you strengthen your belief in yourself.

✓ Every morning when you wake up, look in the mirror and say something positive about yourself every day.

✓ Write down one thing that you can do today to take a small step towards creating a winning life.

✓ Read the Bible verse _Philippians 1: 6_, let this scripture serve as a reminder that God has already started a good work in you.

Principle #2.
Take Control of Your Thought Life

The mind is like a battlefield, with negative thoughts trying to infiltrate our minds to undermine our confidence and hope and distract us from focusing on what matters most. If we are not mindful, these negative thoughts can eat away at our self-esteem and cause us to become discouraged and defeated. This is why you must be adamant about taking control of your thought life.

The most effective way to do this is by taking your thoughts captive. When you take a thought captive you make the choice to be in control of your thoughts, rather than allowing your mind to dwell in negativity. This starts by paying close attention to the kinds off thoughts that run through your head throughout the course of the day. The next step is to replace negative mindsets with self-affirming beliefs that build you up with confidence and inspire you to rise above a poor self-image.

Each of us has an internal dialogue that goes on inside of our heads. This internal dialogue is so powerful that it can either inspire us with hope or hinder us with feelings of inadequacy. Is your thought life empowering you or holding you back? This is an important question to ask yourself because your inner dialogue will either serve as your inner coach inspiring you to rise or it will serve as your inner critic keeping you down.

Without even thinking about it, we talk to ourselves all day every day. For most people, this self-talk is negative. What's more is these inner conversations become part of our reoccurring internal narrative that can prevent us from pursuing our dreams and operating at maximum capacity.

Here's an example of how a negative inner dialogue can work against you: You see someone who is successful and living their dreams. Instead of feeling inspired by them you become envious and you begin to compare yourself unfavorably by saying things like: *I'll never be as successful as so and so. Or, I'm not smart enough, good looking enough or connected enough to live the life that I desire.* By feeding into negative thinking, you rob yourself of the necessary internal inspiration to step into your own success. The other piece is if you continue to allow negative thoughts to run rampant through your mind, your own self-limiting beliefs will become the greatest hindrance to your success.

How do you turn this round? By taking control of your thought life. While you cannot control every single, solitary thought that randomly pops into your mind, you can certainly choose not to dwell on the thoughts that bring you down and undermine your self-worth. The worst thing that you can do to yourself is sit around all day dwelling on negative thoughts and focusing on everything that's wrong with your life. Instead, focus on your plans and dreams. Think about how you are going to create the life you want.

Make it a habit to say at least three positive things to yourself each day. You can say something like: *I am headed for success. The good things that I am seeking are also seeking me. I am blessed and highly favored. I am wired to win.* The lesson here is to take control of your thought life so that your internal dialogue becomes one that inspires you to pursue your dreams and strive for your goals.

Questions for You To Give Some Thought To

Following are some questions designed to get you thinking about ways to shift your inner dialogue to one that will empower you to win.

- On average, is your thought life empowering you or bringing you down? If it tends to bring you down, jot down one small thing that you can do to start stripping the negative voice inside your head of its power?

- Sometimes it can be difficult to feel confident and think highly of ourselves if we haven't made fruitful thinking a priority. What would your life look like if you were more intentional about cultivating a fruitful thought life *(even if you had to go through the motions until you started to wholeheartedly believe it)?* How would you feel? How would you carry yourself? What could you achieve?

- What actions have you been afraid to take, now or in the past, because you thought you could not do it? What steps can you take to give yourself the motivation to take action in the areas of your life where you need to make a change?

- What are three things that you absolutely love about yourself?

Action Steps

✓ Negative thoughts not only affect your mindset, mood & attitude they also affect your body too. Every cell in your body is affected by the thoughts you think. From a health standpoint, you cannot afford to dwell on the negative. Here's an exercise: Write down every negative thought you have about yourself. Next to each negative thought write down at least 2 positive, reaffirming statements to counteract each negative thought.

✓ Each day say at least one scripture that speaks to your identity as a child of God or you can say a positive affirmation daily.

✓ Monitor your internal dialogue. Be vigilant about eliminating thoughts that keep you feeling discouraged and defeated.

✓ Read the Bible verse *2 Corinthians 10: 5*, let this scripture serve as a reminder that you have the power to take control of your thought life.

Principle #3.
Decide What You Want To So That You Can Have A Clearer Picture of Your Goals

What's the one thing that you want in life more than anything else? What's the one thing that would make you happier, more fulfilled and more contented on the inside? No matter what you want to do, be or have in life the process of attaining it starts by deciding what you want, then creating a plan to get it.

If you want your life to feel purposeful and on target, then you have to be able to answer the question: *What do I really want out of life?* Not only do you need to answer this question, but you need to do so in clear, vivid detail. The clearer you identify what you truly want out of life, the better able you will be to come up with a plan for attaining it.

People who are often no more talented or skilled than others, but who take the time to clearly identify what they want, usually end up getting it. Why? Because they choose clarity and purposeful planning over simply winging it & going with the flow. What's more, they make up their minds to dedicate their time, and focus to the attainment of their goals. And when obstacles come their way, they make up their minds to overcome them or work around them. People who are clear about what they want, wire themselves to win by being focused and decisive, no matter the challenges they face.

Although deciding what you want is the single most important step in living the life you desire, most people get stuck at this critical stage. Why? Because, they can't see how the life they want is possible they allow limited vision and lack of clarity to cause them to waver through life. Don't sabotage yourself this way. Don't worry if you don't have all the pieces pulled together just yet, or if you can't figure out how the life you want is possible. Simply start where you are with the resources you have. You will figure out the rest as you move forward.

It's not so important that you have all your ducks lined up in a row. What is most important at this stage is that you have an idea of what you want, and you take the first step then the next to get there. Taking the first step provides you with the necessary momentum to move your life in the direction of your most heartfelt desires and truest goals.

The way the mind works is you must first decide what you want, then your mind will figure out a way to help you get it. Once you firmly decide what you want, you will begin to attract the people, resources and ideas that will enable you to achieve the things you long to achieve.

Spend some time thinking about what you want out of life. Write it down. Then start taking steps in the direction of your goals.

Questions for You To Give Some Thought To

Following are some questions designed to get you thinking about what you really want out of life.

- What do you really want out of life? If you could create your ideal life, what would it look like? What would you be doing?
- What does success mean to you? What do you want your future to look like? With this in mind, complete the following sentences.
  - ➢ Success to me means…
  - ➢ I feel most successful when I…
  - ➢ Three things that I need to do to feel more successful are…
  - ➢ In order to position myself for greater success, here are some changes that I need to make…
  - ➢ If I am not mindful, these are the beliefs, habits, situations and people that can get in the way of my success…

Action Steps

- ✓ Identify what you really want out of life. Think about every area of your life: family, career, personal development, health, finances and relationships. Put some serious thought into what you want for yourself in each of these areas. Write your answers down in a notebook or journal.
- ✓ Create a top 5 want list. Write down the top 5 things you want to do, be and have within the next six months, by this time next year, & within five years. Now write down 5 things

19

you want to do, be and have before you die. Select one item from each list and write down the steps you'll need to take to bring your goals into fruition.

✓ Once upon a time you believed in yourself. You thought you could be anything, do anything, have anything. Reclaim that part of you – your inner child – the part of you that used to have high hopes, big plans and lofty dreams. Identify 3 strong qualities you had as a child. Think about how you can recover some of these qualities. Then, use them as a springboard to become more intentional about creating the life you want.

✓ Pick up a decorative photo album. You should be able to find one for about $5 to $10 at your local Dollar store. Start looking around for positive affirmations, mottos and scriptures that speak about success, dreams and vision. Cut them out and place them in your photo album. Whenever you're in need of a little inspiration, open up your photo album & read your favorite statements.

✓ Read the Bible verse _Psalm 16: 8_, let this scripture serve as a reminder of the importance of not being shaken once you set a plan in motion.

Principle #4.
Start Where You Are

The reason so many people get stuck in a rut and neglect to move forward on their good ideas and dreams is because they overanalyze the idea to the point of analysis paralysis instead of just making a decision and taking action on the idea. Believe it or not, you can analyze a situation so obsessively that your own hyper-analytical inclinations can prevent you from taking action. Don't hold yourself back this way. Stop waiting for everything to be perfect before you take the first step. Simply make a decision to go for it and start where you are.

Whenever I think about the principle of starting where you are, I am reminded of the biblical story in the book of Exodus where God calls on Moses and informs him that he will be leading the Israelites out of Egypt. This was a big and scary task. Pharaoh was a powerful enemy. And Moses felt like he was not prepared or equipped for the task. He pleaded with God to let him off the hook. He made all sorts of excuses as to why he was not prepared. He even told God that because of his speech that no one would listen to him. However, God did not allow Moses' fear of failure or apprehension about whether he was ready to prevent him from fulfilling the task that he was destined to carry out. God simply asked Moses, "What do you have in your hand?" Moses replied, "A shepherd's staff." God used the shepherd's staff to give Moses the confidence and courage he needed to carry out the task.

The powerful lesson that I take from this story is the only way to get started on your goals is to start where you are with the resources you have in hand. With this in mind: What ordinary things do you have on hand right now to help you get started? – a library to start the research, a pen and notebook to write your ideas down, a computer, a good friend you can bounce ideas off of, a voice to start talking to people about your plans a car or bus fare to get out of the neighborhood for a while so that you can think clearly, your children to motivate you to aim higher? As you can see, you already have the basic resources to get started. *So why not start now?*

It's easy to assume that you cannot begin working towards your dreams until every "**i**" is dotted, every "**t**" is crossed, and all your ducks are lined up in a row. But the truth is you can get started on your success right now if you choose to start where you are. As long as you've got a sound mind and a heartfelt desire to live your dreams then you've got the prerequisites to get started. Today, make the decision to start where you are …then, take a leap of faith.

Questions for You To Give Some Thought To

Following are some questions designed to get you thinking about how you can start where you are.

- What talents and resources have you buried or cast aside because you didn't think they were valuable? Could they be valuable and marketable now? How can you build on these things?
- Who or what are you blaming for not getting started on your success? Now that you know that you can start where you are, when are you going to get started?

Action Steps

✓ Make a list of the resources you have on hand. Include things like: time, talent, good health, education, training, special skills, friends, hobbies, family and so on. Consider how you might be able to make the most of these resources so you can move forward on your success journey.

✓ Make a list of all the people you know who can help or support you in any way. Reach out to them and ask for their support. Be prepared with at least 2 to 3 ways that you can be a supportive asset to them.

✓ Read the Bible verse *Zechariah 4: 10*, let this scripture serve as a reminder of the importance of starting small so that you can just begin.

Principle #5.
Run Your Own Race

One of the most counterproductive things that any of us can do to ourselves is to live our lives trying to keep up with other people. Trying to keep up with the Jones's is like trying to win a race by focusing on all the other runners instead of pacing yourself to run your own race. This type of thinking can knock you off your game. Comparing yourself to others takes up a lot of mental energy that could be better spent nurturing your gifts and focusing on your goals.

If we are honest, most people at some point have looked at someone else's life and thought: *If only I had what they had my life would be so much better.* However, the problem with comparing ourselves to others is none of us truly knows what the next man or woman went through or gave up in order to get where they are. Even when you think you know an individual's personal journey, you never truly know what goes on behind the closed doors of their lives. You never know what personal struggles that person had to endure, how they feel in their private moments, what losses they suffered or what obstacles they had to overcome.

Here's the other thing about success: Success comes in many forms like: a successful marriage, healthy, well-adjusted children, having positive relationships with people who care about you, good health, internal joy and peace of mind. So, as you can see, success comes in many forms.

It's important to remember that whenever you measure your life against someone else's you'll always come up short. Because the only true measure of your success is the measurement you make against your own potential. Learn to appreciate and celebrate who you are in your own right. Celebrate the personal achievements you've made. Stop worrying about what other people have. Their journey is not your journey and your journey is not theirs.

Trying to keep up with the Jones's is like drinking from a never-ending cup of envy and covetousness. It sets you up to never be satisfied with your own life. And, when you do make milestones, it will never be enough, because your own envy will prevent you from appreciating your own blessings. So before you drive yourself crazy obsessing over what other people have, always remember that *everything that glitters ain't gold*. The guy at the office who wears the expensive suits and drives the luxury car may be one paycheck away from homelessness. The guy who is juggling several women may also be juggling several STD's or several child support payments. The beautiful woman who all the other women secretly hate may be so lonely that no amount of attention or adulation will ever satisfy that emptiness that she feels on the inside. The point that I am making here is that it is pointless to obsess over what other people have, because you honestly don't know the price they paid to get it.

Today try to be a little more patient with yourself and focus on the good in your life and the positive changes you are making for progress, then sooner than you know it your life will come together too. Today, be thankful for what you have. Go at your own pace and run your own race.

Questions for You To Give Some Thought To

Following are some questions designed to help you appreciate your own life.

- What milestones have you made over the past year?
- Are there areas of success and progress in your life where you do not give yourself enough credit? What are you going to do to change this?

Action Steps

✓ Make a list of at least 2 things that you've got going for yourself. Start noticing areas in your life where you are making progress.

✓ Broaden your definition of success so that it is not limited to money and status.

✓ Read the Bible verse *1 Corinthians 9: 24*, let this scripture serve as a reminder of the importance of running your own race.

Principle #6.
Put Your Goals On Paper

One of the most effective strategies for achieving all of your life's ambitions is to write your goals down. It's important to set goals that inspire you to grow personally and professionally. It's even more important that you write your goals down. Writing your goals down trains your subconscious mind to keep a mental record of your future plans and the good ideas that you have that need a little tweaking before you act on them.

Your ultimate success relies on having and achieving concrete measurable goals. Be they personal, family, financial or professional goals, it is key to your success that you become clear and intentional about where you want to end up in life and what road you need to take to get there. Clarity allows you to do two things: 1.) figure out whether you are directing your time and energy in the right direction 2.) measure your progress.

No matter how you cut it, goals are necessary. Goals help you get from where you are now to where you want to be.

Experts in the psychology of achievement say that your goals should be as specific and measurable as possible so that your subconscious mind can mentally store the information for future reference and hone-in on the experiences and opportunities that will help you succeed. For example: If you have a goal of losing weight, instead of saying *My goal is to lose weight.* The way to turn this vague goal into a clear measurable goal would be to say: *I will lose five pounds in 30 days.* You can also expand on your goal by writing down how you plan achieve it. *I will lose five pounds in 30 days by exercising for 30 minutes each day and eating a well-balanced diet that is low in fat and refined sugars.* Then, write it down.

When you write down your goals, don't be afraid to set goals that stretch you. If you are going to take your life to the next level, then you've got to enlarge your vision of what's possible for you.

With this idea in mind, here is a 9-step goal strategy.

Step. 1 Decide What You Want To Do, Be & Have In This Life.
Set goals for every area of your life. Decide what you want to achieve, accomplish and contribute in the various areas of your life both personally and professionally. Give some serious thought to what you want for yourself in each of these areas. Write your answers down.

Step. 2 Set A Deadline For Each Goal.
The subconscious mind responds to dates and deadlines. The more specific the deadline, the more likely you'll be to reach your target. Think of a deadline as an estimated completion date based on your current skills, knowledge and resources. If you don't reach your goal by the

estimated deadline, take inventory of your skills and resources then adjust your deadline accordingly.

Step. 3 Identify Potential Obstacles and Challenges.
Consider some of the potential obstacles and challenges that might interfere with your goals. Identify the things that are going on inside of you or around you that may create interference or cause a barrier in some way. For every obstacle that you've identified, come up with a strategy to overcome or work around it.

Step 4 Identify The Knowledge, Skills and Personal Traits Needed To Achieve Your Goals
If you are going to achieve something you've never achieved before, you are going to have to learn, do or become something or someone new. Identify the things in your life that you need to work on, change or learn to achieve your goals.

Step. 5 Identify The People, Groups and Organizations That Can Help You Achieve Your Goals.
Who do you know that can help you the most? What can you offer in return to make it a give & give relationship? Perhaps you know someone who has the skills to fine-tune your resume and you'd like their input, what can you offer in return, so that you are adding value to their lives and not just taking from them?

Step 6. Organize Your Goals By Priority
Start with the goal that will have the greatest impact on all your other goals. Is there one goal that will help you accomplish all your other plans faster? If the answer is yes, then that goal should be your #1 priority where you put most of your time, energy and resources into. Organize all your other goals around your primary goal. To do this, you need to know: Which goals need to be completed first and by when? Are there any goals that are dependent upon you accomplishing another goal in a different area? Write this all down.

Step 7. Do Something Each Day That Moves You In The Direction of Your Goals.
Every day, no matter how small do something that moves you in the direction of your goals. Don't let procrastination and complacency kick in. Set a regularly scheduled time to do at least one thing that will aide you in the achievement of your plans. Read an article, make a cold call, practice a skill. They key is to get in the habit of doing something each day that moves you in the direction of your goals.

Step 8. Visualize Yourself Achieving Your Goals.
See yourself achieving your goals. Let yourself feel the feelings that come with achieving your goals. Dig deep and emotionally experience the feelings of excitement, passion, satisfaction and accomplishment as you achieve your goals. See yourself clearly and vividly. Better yet, get

yourself some poster board and make a vision board consisting of pictures, words and images that capture the essence of your plans and dreams.

Step 9. Develop An Obsession For Winning.

It's been said that the authors of the Chicken Soup for The Soul Series, sent their first book out to several publishers and got rejected by every one of them. However, no matter how many rejection letters they received, they kept sending out their manuscript until one day, a publisher signed them and now they rest is history. The authors now sit on a multi-million-dollar publishing empire and are reaping the rewards of their persistence.

It's important for you to believe in yourself even if nobody else believes in you. Sometimes other people are just too narrow-minded in their thinking to see your vision. Don't allow someone else's short-sightedness to cause you to cut your dreams short. You just never know when your break is going to come. If you give up too soon, you may throw your dream down the drain. Never give up on yourself. No matter what obstacles come your way, always remember that he who stays in the race eventually gets to the finish line.

Questions for You To Give Some Thought To

Following are some questions designed to get you thinking about your goals.

- What good ideas do you have in the back of your mind that if tweaked can be turned into achievable goals?
- What small steps can you take to move yourself closer to your goals?

Action Steps

✓ Think about one goal that you want to accomplish. Write it down and complete one action toward this goal by the end of the week.
✓ Pair up with another goal-oriented individual and become a support system for one another.
✓ Read the Bible verse *Proverbs 21: 5*, let this scripture serve as a reminder of the importance of being a diligent planner especially concerning your goals in life.

Principle #7.
Focus On Your Focus

What do I mean by the phrase ...*focus on your focus?* It means to focus on what matters most to you in every situation. When you focus on what matters most you are training yourself to focus on your purpose and destiny. A clear sense of purpose is essential to your success. Without a clear sense of purpose, it's easy to become distracted and end up wasting a lot of time on people, things and situations that do not serve where you are trying to go and what you are seeking to do with your life. Without a clear sense of purpose, you can end up putting a lot of misdirected energy and effort into situations that do not align with what you are trying to achieve.

A story is told of a young man passing through a small town on his way to a big city. Accidentally, he made a wrong turn and ended up off course. After driving several miles trying to find his way back to the main highway, he stopped by a local coffee shop. As the waitress got ready to take his order, he said "I think I'm lost and I need to get back on the main highway." The waitress smiled at the young man and asked, "Do you know where you are?" The young man replied, "I'm not sure, but I know where I'm going." The waitress finished taking his order and said: "Young man, you are not lost you just need a little direction." She then told the young man how to get back on the main highway.

Believe it or not, many people end up on the wrong road just like this young man because they do not have a roadmap to guide them on their journey. As a result, they end up off course feeling like something is missing from their lives. And since they do not have a real sense of purpose, they aimlessly flutter through life feeling lost and misdirected. Many people do not get what they want out of life, not because they do not have the talent or capability to do so. It's because they do not have a clear sense of purpose and they allow themselves to focus on the petty.

Your life is like a journey. Your purpose is the compass that guides you on that journey. When you do not focus on your purpose, you end up investing a lot of time, energy and resources in a direction that is not consistent with your ultimate outcome.

Here's another important aspect of purpose: Your purpose is not limited to your career. It's not what other people say you should do with your life. Your purpose is not defined by past failures or previous mistakes. Your purpose is defined by you, by your deepest desires and heartfelt longings. It's the *"Why?"* behind everything you do. Your purpose answers the questions: *Why am I here? What do I believe I was put on this earth to do?*

One of the major contributing factors to your success is clarity of purpose. When you are clear about why you are here, you can honor your purpose, wherever you go, in whatever industry you work in and in any job you hold.

It's important that you spend a little time each day thinking about your purpose, until it is so crystal clear that everything you do incorporates your purpose.

It's important for you to know that every person on the planet is born with a purpose. Further, each of us is equipped with an internal compass that naturally guides us in the direction of our purpose. When you uncover your purpose and direct all your activities around it, you become more fruitful. Plus, you'll be able to identify the things in your life that no longer fit with where you are trying to go. When you are truly on purpose, you will feel a deep sense of fulfillment. What's more, the opportunities, and resources that you'll need will naturally gravitate your way. What seems like a coincidence or chance opportunity will be life's way of moving you in the direction of your purpose.

Defining your central purpose in life is about taking some time to put some thought into what really matters to you, what you feel called or led to do and what gives your life meaning. Begin by identifying your strengths, talents, personality traits and aspirations. Then, ask yourself: *Why am I here? How can I contribute my time and talents to make the world a better place in my own unique way?* Even if your contribution starts right in your own home, your block or your community, what matters most is that you begin to live your life with a greater sense of purpose. Living with purpose enables you to leave a legacy that will extend beyond your lifespan.

Sometimes it can be difficult to uncover your purpose because most people think of purpose as a larger than life mission. But if you could try to think in terms of the little things you do each day that give your life greater meaning and that help others in some small way, you will begin to uncover the path to your purpose. Spend some time thinking about your purpose. Then be purposeful in all that you do.

Questions for You To Give Some Thought To

Following are some questions designed to get you thinking about your purpose.

- Sometimes to figure out your purpose, you've got to go back to your childhood for clues. What kinds of things did you enjoy as a child? Do you find yourself doing any of these things today? Do you remember anything that came naturally to you as a child that you are still drawn to today?
- Are there any dreams that you've laid to rest because you've bought into the notion that once you become an adult it's time to put childhood dreams away? Is there anything that you can do now to recover some of your lost dreams, even if you do it as a hobby?
- What are your strengths? What are your talents? What do other people say you're good at? What do others call on you to do or help them with? What do you find yourself doing because it comes second nature to you? What

do you find yourself doing in your spare time? What do you find yourself daydreaming about? What's the one thing you would do if you knew you could not fail?

- If money was not an issue, what would you be doing right now? If money was not an issue, what would you devote most of your time to?
- If you found out that you only had one year to live, what 3 things would you want to do before you die? What's stopping you from doing them now?
- What will people see with their eyes when you are living with a greater sense of purpose? What will they say about you?
- When your time is up and you meet the Creator, what do you want God to say about how you lived your life?

Action Steps

✓   Identify your purpose on the smallest level by noticing the things in life that inspire, intrigue or interest you in some small way or that just seem to naturally fit with your strengths and personality.

✓   Another way to gain clarity around your purpose is to write out a life purpose statement. Spend some time thinking about your purpose. Then, write it down in the form of a one sentence statement. As an example, here's my purpose statement: *My life purpose is to motivate and inspire others to live their best lives through teaching, speaking and writing.*

✓   Ask yourself: *What is my purpose? Why am I here? How can I contribute to mankind in my own unique way?* Allow your answers to serve as a guide to uncovering your purpose.

✓   Take a few moments to write down a sentence or two defining your purpose. Complete the following sentence. *My purpose is...*

_____

_____

_____

_____

_____

_____

_____

_____

_____

_____

_____

_____

✓ Read the Bible verse *Ephesians 2: 10*, let this scripture inspire you to remind yourself that you were created with a purpose.

Principle #8.
Cultivate Healthy Self-Esteem

Did you know that your self-esteem affects every aspect of your life? ...from your relationships, boundaries and habits to how confidently you go after your goals & dreams. Your self-esteem also affects how you respond to life's challenges and setbacks. A healthy sense of self-esteem is critical to your success because it's difficult to achieve long lasting success and personal fulfillment if you have a low opinion of yourself and lack the confidence to go after the things you want in life.

Our self-esteem is influenced by many factors such as: family upbringing, our experiences, childhood trauma, media messages and our own beliefs and expectations. With all these factors that affect our self-esteem the 3 most important things that you can do to cultivate healthy self-esteem are: monitor your self-talk, replace self-defeating beliefs with self-affirming ones and do something daily that strengthens your confidence.

It's important for you to know that nobody feels 100% confident all the time. Not even the people who seem like they are super confident. Everyone has moments of self-doubt and insecurity. But, what separates people with healthy self-esteem from those with poor self-esteem is people with healthy self-esteem don't let their insecurities prevent them from striving for the things they want in life.

The mind works in such a way, that it believes whatever we tell it regularly. If you routinely feed your mind a mental diet of negative thoughts, your mind will begin to believe these negative ideas and suggestions. As a result, you may start making choices based on insecurity and a low opinion of yourself instead of making choices based on who you truly are at the core of your spirit.

The opposite is also true. If you feed your mind a regular diet of affirming, empowering ideas, over time you'll start to improve your self-esteem level. Plus, when you develop a more positive belief system, you'll be more inclined to pursue your goals with greater confidence and faith.

The Bible has a lot to say about who you truly are at the core of your being and what you have the capacity to do, become and achieve as a child of God. Knowing what the Bible has to say about you is an absolute game-changer. Because knowing who you truly are empowers you to tap your unrealized potential, nurture your gifts and see yourself in a more powerful, positive light. This attitude of confidence, faith and hope will bring out the best in you and propel you to rise and thrive no matter what life brings your way.

Always remember that how far you go in life and how happy you are depend, to a large extent, on how much you believe in yourself and how forcefully you act on your beliefs. If success and personal fulfillment are your ultimate goals, you cannot afford to not be proactive about maintaining a healthy level of self-esteem.

Questions for You To Give Some Thought To

Following are some questions designed to get you thinking about ways to boost your self-esteem.

- Do you have a healthy sense of self-esteem? If not, what would it take for you to feel better about yourself? To feel more confident and empowered on the inside?
- A big part of self-esteem involves liking yourself. With this in mind, what do you like about yourself? Identify at least ten things.
- Another contributing factor to healthy self-esteem involves knowing what your core strengths are. With this in mind, what are your core strengths? What are you good at? If you are not sure, what do other people say that you're good at? What do other people come to you for help with or ask your advice about most often?
- Are there areas in your life where you are overly critical of yourself or where you do not give yourself enough credit? What are you going to do to change this?
- Who or what are you blaming for your level of self-esteem? Now that you know that you are responsible for maintaining your self-esteem, what are you going to do to build yourself up from the inside out?

Action Steps

✓ Make a list of three things that you are proud of.
✓ Every morning when you wake up, look in the mirror and say something positive about yourself. Do this as often as you need to until you pump yourself up with the confidence you need to build unbreakable self-esteem.
✓ Build relationships with positive people who positively impact your life.
✓ Sometimes our confidence can become eroded by the obstacles that we encounter in life. The most effective way to deal with an obstacle is to brainstorm ways to get around, over or through it. For every obstacle that you encounter or could potentially encounter, come up with three different ways of handling it. There is always at least one way to deal with an obstacle, you just have to spend some time thinking about it.
✓ Write down at least three more things that you can do to increase your level of self-esteem.
✓ Read the Bible verse _Psalm 139: 14_, let this scripture serve as a reminder that you are fearfully & wonderfully made by God.

Principle #9.
Don't Let the Past Keep You From Moving Forward

The past is a funny thing in that most of us already know that to move forward we need to be able put our past behind us. However most people struggle with moving past their past. Your past can be one of the greatest hurdles in your life. Why? Because, if you are unwilling or unable to put the past behind you, you may allow yourself to become emotionally stuck. As a result, you end up holding yourself back from living your most abundant life. If you are to live your very best life – I'm talking about the kind of life that fulfills you in a major way, then you've got to develop the attitude that no matter what has happened to you in the past that you will not allow it to define or defeat you.

Far too often, we allow painful past experiences to arrest our emotional development. This prevents us from moving forward and getting on with our lives. No matter what has happened to you and how badly you feel about it you are the only one who can turn your life around. You are the only one who can put in the work to make your life better. The past is behind you. The future is yours for the taking. But, it's up to you to choose your path.

Following is a story about a young man named Ricky who allowed his past to keep him from moving forward and it cost him big time. As you read the story see if there are any lessons that you can pull from it.

By the time Ricky was thirteen, he lived in three different foster homes and transferred to four different schools. His father was in and out of jail. His mother died of an overdose.

By the time social services entered the picture, they were able to place his 13-month-old twin sisters with an adoptive family. But, nobody wanted to take on a teenager with his own personality coupled with the residual effects that come from early childhood trauma.

Because Ricky was the oldest, he had the longest memory. He remembered the drinking. He remembered the fights. He remembered the times his father would bring other women home and beat his mother down if she dared to say a word. He remembered the bruises. He remembered the blood. And although, he tried hard to forget, he remembered the times his mother asked him to find a strong enough vein so that he could help her inject the Heroine in her arm without leaving too many visible scars.

By the time Ricky was fifteen, he started running with the wrong crowd. Dabbing in illegal activities. He got busted for drug possession. Served three years in a juvenile detention center and the remainder of his sentence in a minimum security pen. When Ricky was released, he came home angry, with no skills and no support system to help him find his way. Since institutionalized living was all Ricky had ever known, he decided that he could not make it in the free world, so seven months later he landed himself back in jail on a parole violation.

For Ricky he blamed his father's violence, his mother's overdose and being separated from his siblings for causing him to make decisions that kept him from reaching his full potential. Are you like Ricky blaming your past for not living your very best life? If you have had a difficult past and it is causing you to make decisions that keep you in a place of self-defeat, now that you're all grown up what are you going to do to change your life for the better?

When we are children, we have no control over the circumstances that we are born into and no frame of reference to understand why people do the things they do. As children we are not responsible. We did not ask to be born. Nor, can we pick the people who raise us. But once we become adults, we must learn to separate the things that have happened in the past, from the things we now have control over. And as an adult you now have control over your choices. You have control over your actions. And although it takes a great deal of discipline, you also have control over your outlook.

You cannot erase your past. You cannot make people love you, treat you kindly or meet your needs if they are unwilling or unable to do so. But the one thing you can do is take charge of your future.

Each day that you find the resolve to press forward you are changing your life for the better. Each day that you refuse to allow painful events from your past to define, defeat or derail you, you are changing your life for the better.

Today, know that no matter what has happened to you and how badly you feel about it, as long as you've got breath in your body you have the power to change your life for the better.

Questions for You To Give Some Thought To

Following are some questions designed to get you thinking about how to press pass your past.

- Are you allowing your past to keep you from moving forward? What steps can you take to begin putting the past in its proper perspective?
- There is always a cost for holding on to the things in life that prevent us from moving on fully. With this in mind: What is it costing you to stay stuck in the past?

Action Steps

✓ Sometimes it is in the area where we feel the most pain and have the greatest amount of personal struggle that life can use us to help someone else. With this in mind, share your life story with someone who needs to hear your testimony so that you can help them realize that one's past doesn't have to define or defeat them.

✓ Read the Bible verse *Philippians 3: 13-14*, let this scripture serve as a reminder to keep pressing forward.

Principle #10.
Project An Image
That Makes A Positive Impact

The energy and image that we put out to the world has a tremendous impact on how we are perceived and treated by others, not only in business but in every area of our lives. When you take the time to put forth your best energy and image, you're better able to make a positive first impression.

Take a moment and think about someone you know who is greatly respected. What words come to mind when you think of this person? I'll bet the words: confident, competent and credible are somewhere in the mix. Do you think their image came by accident? Probably not. Even if the individual did not think he was consciously crafting his image, he was by way of his attitude, personal presentation and habits.

Projecting an image that communicates confidence, competence and credibility starts with knowing that you have what it takes to make it.

It's important to develop the mindset that you are where you are today, because you've put in the work to get there. This internal attitude of self-assurance will give you the necessary confidence to project your most powerful, positive image.

The second thing that will help you to craft your best image is to consistently ask for feedback. Most people will not voluntarily give you feedback, because they don't want to risk offending you, it never occurred to them to tell you what they truly think about you or they simply do not care. So to get honest and open feedback, you are going to have to ask for it, and make it safe for the individual to tell you how they honestly feel. Some questions you might want to ask are:

1. What was your first impression of me when we first met and what led you to come to that initial impression of me?
2. What adjectives come to mind when you think of me?
3. Is there anything about the way I dress, speak or act that might be holding me back or turning people off?
4. What suggestions would you make in each of the above areas in order for me to project a more powerful, polished image that is consistent with the message I want to communicate to others?

And here's the most important part of handling feedback: There's only one appropriate response and it's "Thank you." Don't get bent out of shape if people give you critical feedback. Remember, you asked for it. Look at feedback as a free coaching session. It's information that you can use to step up your game. With this idea in mind, here are 8 tips that will help you project your most powerful image.

1. Dress for success. Be sure to observe your company's dress code. Make sure that your

clothing, make-up, hair style and accessories send the kind of image that you want to convey.

2. Be the consummate professional. Be professional in your demeanor, attire, behavior as well as your verbal and written communication.

3. Be reliable and be on time. When all else fails all you have is your word. Let your word be your bond.

4. Project a positive attitude. How do you come across to others? What message are you sending through your behavior and body language? How do your bosses, employees and colleagues perceive you? Think positive, speak positive and be positive.

5. Be easy-going. People prefer to be around people who are flexible and who don't make a big deal out of every little minor annoyance. By being easy-going, you'll come across to others as a team player and people will be naturally drawn to you.

6. Handle proprietary information with care. Be the type of person who others can come to when they need guidance or a safe sounding board.

7. Be an attentive listener. When people speak to you, try to focus your complete attention on what the other person is saying.

8. Know how to read people. Reading people is about understanding that people have two faces: The one they present publicly and the private one. Reading people is about seeing

beyond the public face in order to discern a person's true message and motives.

Questions for You To Give Some Thought To

Following are some questions designed to get you thinking about additional ways to project your best image.

- Where can it be said that you need to step it up in order to project your most powerful image?
- Do an honest self-assessment. What areas of your personality, habits and work practices do you need to improve?

Action Steps

✓ Implement one action step from the 9-tip plan.
✓ Read the Bible verse *Matthew 5: 16*, let this scripture remind you to let your light come through in all that you do.

Principle #11.
Use Your Time Wisely

Have you ever taken the time to think about how short life truly is? Time really does fly. And if you are not mindful about how you spend your time, you may come to find that you have wasted far too many years passively allowing life to pass you by.

When you're in your teens and early twenties it seems like you've got all the time in the world. So much so that many youth naively believe that the world is their personal oyster. But as you get a little older and life begins to slow you down a bit you start to realize that time waits for no one, not even you. The lesson here is: If you squander your time, you may live to regret it. When your time is up, it's up, no matter how much unfinished business you have or how many unrealized dreams you never got around to pursuing. This is why it is so important that you make the most of each day by becoming very intentional about how you spend your time.

If you are like most people, I'll bet that there have been times in your life when you've waited until the last minute to complete a task or work on an important project, only to feel rushed and pressured by having to do it in a crunched amount of time. You've probably even made excuses for yourself by saying things like, *I work better under pressure.* But the truth is most people don't, because if you are trying to throw things together at the last-minute wondering whether or not you can pull it off, then you are not working at your optimum level.

I know what you're thinking. You've got a lot on your plate and the last thing you need is another item to add to your already full to-do-list. However, when you plan your schedule it makes your life flow more smoothly. It enables you to manage your days around your most important plans and priorities. As a result, you become more productive and effective.

To become a better task master, determine your priorities. Then manage your time around them. Get yourself a planner that allows you to see the month at-a-glance and that organizes your schedule monthly, weekly and daily. You can do this on paper, your computer, blackberry or iPhone. The key is to develop some kind of time management system.

Take fifteen minutes on Sunday evening or Monday morning to plan your week. Write down the important things you need to do for the week. Once you've planned your schedule, you can adjust it each day as needed.

Be ruthless about eliminating self-imposed time wasters such as: indecision, procrastination, laziness, not writing out your schedule, lack of organization, too much television or allowing yourself to become easily distracted. When you're at work, ask your boss to help you prioritize your work schedule by letting you know which tasks need to be completed first and which ones can wait or be delegated. Whenever you find yourself getting off track, ask yourself: *Is what I'm doing right now the best use of my time?*

Questions for You To Give Some Thought To

Following are some questions designed to get you thinking about how to manage your time wisely.

- Are you managing your time effectively or do you have a tendency to let the day get away from you?
- What steps can you take to better manage your time?

Action Steps

✓ Set priorities. Priorities are about deciding which things are most important to you at this stage in your life. Then, determining which of those things will help you achieve your goals most quickly.

✓ Learn to say no. If saying no is difficult for you, ask yourself: *What will it cost me in time, energy, money, priorities, emotional stress and level of inconvenience to say yes to this?*

✓ Read the Bible verse *Psalm 90: 12*, let this scripture serve as a reminder of the importance of using your time wisely.

Principle #12.
Let Your Highest Values Serve As Your Compass for Life

Values guide every decision you make which means that your values ultimately direct your destiny. If you want to achieve the deepest level of success and personal fulfillment you must know what your highest values are and allow them to serve as your compass for life. If you are not clear about what's most important to you – what you truly stand for, you may find yourself wavering back and forth when it's time to make important decisions instead of decisively determining your course of action.

It goes without saying that your values are the foundation for your life because everything you do and pursue is built around what you value most.

Your values determine every decision you make. So, when you find that you're having difficulty making or sticking to a decision, it usually means that you are not clear about what you value most in that situation.

When you know what your values are, decision-making becomes a lot easier, because your decisions will be based on your highest ideals.

Take some time to clarify your values. To figure out what your values are, ask yourself: "What's most important to me in life?" Is it education? Family? Faith? Health? Spending time with family? Money? Peace? Happiness? Being a good person? Giving back to the community? Building nurturing relationships?

Write your values down in their order of importance, starting with the most important one and ending with the least.

1) _____
2) _____
3) _____
4) _____
5) _____
6) _____
7) _____
8) _____
9) _____
10) _____

When you are finished, review your values and evaluate whether your values are helping you achieve your desired life or hindering you. If a value is hindering you, reevaluate that value. Then, adopt a new value that aligns with the life you desire.

Sometimes it can be difficult to get a clear picture of your highest values because in today's social-media driven culture we are so inundated with messages that seek to sell us on what's important. However, only you can decide which values are important to you. You and you alone determine your values. Always remember that your values, whatever they might be, are the motivating guidelines that drive your life's path.

Questions for You To Give Some Thought To

Following are some questions designed to get you thinking about your values.

- If a good year blimp were to fly across the sky with a banner describing 3 things that you stand for, what would it say & why?
- If you could spend one day with any person who ever lived who would it be and why?
- If you could have one prayer answered, what would it be and why?
- Describe a time when you felt really strong about a cause or issue. What do you think this says about your highest values?
- Your high school newspaper tracked you down and asked if they could do a story on you, what would you want the headline of your story to be? What does your desired headline say about your values?
- If you could solve one problem for the world what would it be and why?

Action Steps

- ✓ Review your values list again. What does your list reveal to you? Put some thought into how your values are directing your life's path.
- ✓ Know that you can change your life in an instant by changing your values. For example, if money was your number one value but you feel like you've been chasing the wrong kind of success, you can change

your life by changing that value. Instead of money being your number one value, perhaps you can move it down the list and place health or fulfilling relationships higher on your list of values.

✓ You can always tell what a person values most by how they spend their time and what they talk about most often. Spend some time thinking about where you spend most of your time and what you talk about most often. This is an indication of what you value most.

✓ Read the Bible verse *Proverbs 21: 3*, let this scripture serve as a reminder of the importance of being the type of person who does what is just and right.

Principle #13.
Connect With Positive People Who Want To See You Win

One of the most critical components of success is having people around you who want to see you win – people who are happy for you whenever you make strides and who support you in your goals. People you can bounce ideas off of and who you can share your plans, dreams and struggles with. It's even better if you can be part of a dream team. A dream team consists of two or more people who come together on a regular basis, either in person, over the telephone or via email to support each other's plans and goals, brainstorm ways to accomplish these plans and share helpful resources.

The purpose of a dream team is to serve as a supportive network for one another. You can organize your dream team around a single issue such as: entrepreneurship, financial empowerment or a social cause that you believe in. Or, you can simply come together around any and every issue that you would like support with.

It's important to understand that no one is an island. You can only go so far alone. You need to connect with other positive people who want to see you succeed and who will encourage you to take steps toward your goals.

For years I have been part of a dream team. Some of my best work and biggest breakthroughs both personally and professionally came from these powerful alliances. Some of the members of my dream team have started businesses, others advanced their careers. Still others learned important life lessons that have helped them in their personal endeavors. I cannot stress enough how valuable a dream team is. You can only go so far alone. Let a dream team help you take your life to the next level. Surround yourself with people who not only want you to win but who want you to win big.

Here's the final piece: Be willing to help other people along the way. You cannot expect people to support and assist you, if you are not willing to support and assist other people as well. Think of ways that you can be of service and add value to the lives of others. Whether it's through encouragement, sharing resources and opportunities or making a referral, be willing to invest in another person's success as well.

As a lone wolf it is virtually impossible to succeed, but when you consistently help other people, you create a circle of support where everyone contributes to one another's success. The best part of it all is when you win, everyone in your circle wins, because you are all pulling together and supporting each other's dreams. This is a critical component to your success.

Questions for You To Give Some Thought To

Following are some questions designed to get you thinking about ways to connect with people who want you to win.

- Who are some of the most positive people you know? What can you do to develop more mutually beneficial relationships with them?
- Who can assist you in achieving your goals, both personally and professionally? What do you need to do to build relationships with them?
- What associations, groups or organizations can you join to connect with like-minded, positive people?

Action Steps

✓ Identify four to six people that you can recruit for your dream team. If you don't know four to six people, start with one other person and build from there.

✓ Identify your team's purpose. Decide how often you're going to meet and where. Will you meet in person, over the phone or set up a time to correspond online. If possible, try to carve out 60 to 90-minutes each week to meet.

✓ Make sure that each member is committed to helping one another succeed and grow by sharing ideas, support, contacts and information.

✓ Take the dream team meetings seriously. Be on time and treat it like any other priority in your life.

✓ Read the Bible verse *Proverbs 27: 17*, let this scripture serve as a reminder of the importance of connecting with people who can sharpen you.

Principle #14.
Don't Let Negative People Rain On Your Parade

Negative people can drain your energy, and erode your confidence, if you let them. How? Because when you are constantly on the receiving end of negative, belittling and condescending comments, over time, it can cause your own levels of optimism to drop.

One of the worst feelings in the world is having someone dismiss your dreams and try to tear you down with sarcasm, indifference or blatant hostility. The time and energy that it takes to dodge or deal with a toxic person's negativity can take a toll on your own self-esteem and wellbeing. Even more, it can discourage you to the point where you stop believing in yourself and end up giving up on your dreams. This is why it's critical that you keep negative people as far away from you and your dreams as possible. It's even more important that you build yourself up so much on the inside that their negative comments do not steal your joy or cause you to become just as toxic as them.

It's been said that the people in your life do one of three things: They lift you up, keep you where you are or bring you down. Unfortunately, the more you want to do with your life the more mindful you've got to be about who you allow in it. So the question is: Are the people in your life lifting you up, keeping you where you are or bringing you down? Spend some time thinking about this question because the company you keep can have a major impact on how you feel about yourself, which can ultimately impact your success.

Remember that every successful person has critics. Everyone with a dream has people who cannot see their vision. Everyone who is doing something positive with their lives has to deal with people who try to rain on their parade. So don't be discouraged by the nay-sayers and dream slayers. In fact, one of the most effective ways to deal with negative people is to turn their negative criticism into feedback that you can use to step up your game even more.

As unfortunate as it is to deal with, negative people come with the territory. Just build up your confidence, develop a thick skin and if all else fails allow your haters to serve as your motivators. Always remember that in the end no matter what people have to say about you, their words hold no power because you are the only one who has the final word on your dreams.

Questions for You To Give Some Thought To

Following are some questions designed to get you thinking about ways to handle negative people.

- Are there people in your life who are part of your inner circle who need to be moved to you acquaintance circle?

- Sometimes people stay in friendships that they have outgrown in an effort to convince themselves that they have not changed. Is there anyone who you are still friends with or trying to take with you even though it's clear by their actions that they are not remotely invested in your success? What is this friendship costing you?
- Have you ever had a negative person try to crush your dreams? How did you handle it?
- Who are you listening to that you need to stop listening to?

Action Steps

✓ Turn your haters into your motivators. Instead of allowing yourself to become beaten down by negative criticism, use it to motivate you to step up your game even more.
✓ Prove your critics wrong by becoming even more determined to accomplish your plans and dreams.
✓ Read the Bible verse *1 Corinthians 15: 33*, let this scripture serve as a reminder to be mindful of the company that you keep.

Principle #15.
Keep At It

For years successful men and women have understood the phrase: *Every step counts*. These three simple words pack a lot of power, because every step that you take in the direction of your goals has an accumulative effect towards them. The longer you work at your goals and the more effort you put into the achievement of your dreams, the greater your chances of accomplishing your goals. The problem with most people is not that they don't have the skill or talent. It's that they don't have the staying power to stick with something long enough to see if it's truly fruitful. Instead, they give up at the first sign of struggle.

Every effort that you make towards the things you want in life is like making a deposit in your success account. Over time no matter how small your efforts, your account will begin to pay interest in the form of a completed task, or an accomplished goal.

Your progress in life is directly related to how much sustained effort you put into your goals. If you read or watch biographies of successful people, even the ones who appear to be an overnight success, you will find that they stayed the course no matter how many obstacles came their way. Even more, they did something on a regular basis to move themselves closer to their goals. Here's the biggest part, whenever they were knocked down, they dusted themselves off and got back up. On a daily basis you should ask yourself: *What can I do today to move myself closer to my goals?*

Questions for You To Give Some Thought To

Following are some questions designed to get you thinking about how to develop your staying power.

- What small things can you do on a regular basis to get yourself into the habit of practicing sustained effort?
- What can you do to keep yourself motivated if you start to lose momentum?

Action Steps

✓ Take five minutes right now to make a mental note of one small thing that you will do first thing tomorrow morning to get yourself in the habit of practicing sustained effort.
✓ Work to increase your momentum. Develop the characteristic of persistence.
✓ Read the Bible verse *Galatians 6: 9*, let this scripture serve as a reminder to not give up and keep on keeping on.

Principle #16.
Take An Honest Look At Your Financial Situation & Habits

We cannot talk about success in life without talking about finances. Because no matter what your goals are in life, whether you want to go back to school, purchase a home, provide a comfortable life for your family or retire comfortably, these things all require money.

So, the question I pose to you is this: At your current position and salary, can you afford to live the lifestyle that you truly want? I'm not talking about being able to buy a sports car, a million-dollar home or a vacation in the most exquisite resort in Monaco. I'm merely asking whether you have the financial freedom to pay your bills on time, stay out of debt and pursue some of your dreams or at least many of the items on your wish list, without feeling pressured to just get by.

If you are drowning in debt, or if your current salary cannot sustain your basic needs and some of your desires, it will be difficult to feel in control of your life. This is why you must take the time to plan and understand your finances.

This includes sitting down with pen and paper in hand and identifying how much income comes in and out each month. Second, seriously think about how much you want to earn, save and invest. Third, cut back on the areas where you are overspending. Last but not least, you must honestly assess the career track that you're on in order to figure out if you can survive and thrive on your current salary and whether or not you've positioned yourself to earn at the higher paying ends of your industry.

Financial security means different things to different people, but the quickest way to plan and understand your finances is to write out an operating budget for your household that identifies your monthly income and expenses. Then, put an exact dollar figure on how much you need to earn, save and invest each year in order to live the lifestyle that you desire. So, how much do you want to earn, save and invest? How much do you want to have when you retire? How much money will you need to maintain your current lifestyle when you stop working? How much debt do you owe and what steps do you need to take to get yourself out of debt? If you're a parent, what kind of financial head start do you want to provide for your child?

In order to factor in your financial needs and goals, it's also important that you get a clear picture of your financial habits. Following are ten statements designed to get you thinking about your financial habits. Please read each statement and respond by saying yes or no.

1. *I live within my means.*
2. *I do not make excessive purchases on my credit cards.*
3. *I feel financially secure.*
4. *I pay my credit cards in full.*

5. *I know where my money goes each day.*
6. *I have three to six month's salary saved up in case of an emergency.*
7. *I am hoping that I will meet a wealthy partner who will help make things a little easier for me.*
8. *I always pay my bills on time.*
9. *I contribute to a retirement plan consistently.*
10. *I keep a log of my spending habits.*

Your answers to the questions above should provide you with some insights about your financial habits. If you are satisfied with your responses, keep up the good work. If not, make the necessary changes you need to make in order to better plan and understand your finances.

Questions for You To Give Some Thought To

Following are some questions designed to get you thinking about your finances.

- What are your financial goals for this year?
- What are you doing now to move yourself closer to your financial goals? What else could you be doing?
- How much do you earn each month? Do you overspend in any area? If yes, what areas can you cut back on in order to save some money?
- Examine your attitudes about money. Examine your spending habits. Do you make purchases when you're stressed or sad? Do

you rationalize living beyond your means by saying things like: "I deserve this?" What thoughts and beliefs do you have about money? What have you discovered about yourself as it relates to your spending habits? What are you prepared to do in order to turn your financial situation around?

Action Steps

- ✓ All financial security begins with knowing where your money goes. Over the next three months keep a spending journal. If you are spending more than you are saving, look for areas where you can cut back.
- ✓ Pay yourself first. Take 10% or more of your income and put it aside before you start spending any money. This will guarantee that you will create a financial stream for investing and retirement. If you are not at the point where you can save 10%, save as much as you can. The key is to just start saving. If you get a bonus or a raise, put it into your savings and continue to live on the income you had before. If you haven't already joined your company's retirement plan do so and put the maximum amount in. Have the money directly deposited into your savings account or a mutual fund.
- ✓ Develop an attitude of gratitude. Start paying attention to areas where your life is already prosperous. Be thankful for what you have while creating avenues for more. Notice the

many ways that you are blessed. When you develop an attitude of gratitude an internal shift in your consciousness occurs allowing you to invite more prosperity into your life.

✓ Give back. The cycle of reciprocity is kept in constant motion through giving, because currency is a form of energy. Whether you give to your place of worship, a cause you believe in or those who are less fortunate than you, by giving to those in need you contribute to humanity and keep the cycle of reciprocity in motion. And here's the thing about the cycle of reciprocity: It works both ways. By giving you've set up a channel for money to flow back in your direction when you are in need.

✓ Read the Bible verse *Proverbs 21: 20*, let this scripture serve as a reminder of the necessity of financial planning.

Principle #17.
Curb Your Consumerism

Are you one of those people who just love the sense of excitement that comes from making a new purchase? Driving home in a new vehicle? Or trying on a new dress or suit from your favorite boutique? If you're like most people I'll bet the answer is yes.

Let me ask you another question. *Do you feel that same sense of excitement when the credit card bill arrives?* When you look at your bank statement and notice that your account is rapidly dwindling? When you look at your credit card bill and notice that you owe more than you can realistically pay off each month? See where I'm going here? If your spending habits are costing you more than you can truly afford, then perhaps it's time to curb your consumerism.

It is virtually impossible to turn on your TV, the radio, walk down the street or pick up a newspaper or magazine without reading or hearing about the latest new thing that you need, or the novel gadget that one of your friends or co-workers have and how you need to have it too. Advertising permeates our culture. Although you can monitor some of it, there is no way that you can avoid all of it. But, if you want to avoid becoming broke, then you have to make disciplined choices around how you spend your money. Even more, you cannot allow yourself to become consumed with consumerism.

There comes a point when you need to ask yourself: *Will a bigger TV make me happier when the one that I already have is working just fine? Is the double latte from my favorite gourmet coffee shop that much better than the coffee that I can brew at home? Is eating lunch out every day healthier and more cost effective than bringing my lunch to work?* The bottom and top line is if you want to have a little something stashed away for a rainy day, then you've got to be willing to not only adjust your spending habits but to shift your lifestyle from one that is consumer-driven to one that is centered around being disciplined with your money.

In the book, "*The Millionaire Next Door,*" by Thomas J. Stanley and William D. Danko, the authors studied the habits of first generation self-made millionaires. The common theme that helped them all to build wealth in one generation was their ability to live below their means and to not define themselves by the kind of car they drove, the clothes they wore or the type of house they lived in. While their peers were out buying high status, items getting themselves into deep debt, the millionaires in the aforementioned book thought long and hard before making a major purchase often delaying instant gratification so that they would not incur unnecessary debt.

It was the ability to be disciplined and not worry about keeping up with the Jones's that enabled these millionaires to build wealth instead of recklessly spending their money. What's more, many of these millionaires were in blue collar industries with annual incomes ranging from $40,000 and up. But, because they kept their spending low and invested and saved their money, their income to debt ratio worked in their favor. How? Because at the end of the day, it's not how much money you make that determines your wealth. It's how much money you keep. So the question I pose to you is: *Are you willing to curb your consumerism in order to build long term wealth?*

Questions for You To Give Some Thought To

Following are some questions designed to get you thinking about ways to curb your consumerism.

- What are your buying habits? Do you make purchasing decisions based on your wants or based on your needs? What do your buying habits reveal about how you manage your money? What do your buying habits over the past year reveal about how much you invest and save for the future?

- How many high-status items do you own? (ex: designer shoes and purses, novelty gadgets, luxury cars, etc.) How many investments do you have in relation to your high-status items?

- What does wealth mean to you? What have you done thus far to move yourself closer to your definition of wealth?

- What is one thing that you can do this month to curb your consumerism?

Action Steps

✓ Set weekly, monthly, yearly and lifetime financial goals. People who build wealth are goal oriented. Not only are they goal oriented, but they also keep their financial goals in the forefront of their minds when making purchasing decisions. Put this habit into practice immediately.

✓ Don't try to keep up with the Jones's. Your neighbor remodels his house, you feel you have to remodel yours too. Your best friend blows money like it's water, you feel pressured to do the same. All your coworkers have the latest gadgets, you feel you need the latest gadget too. If you are guilty of this type of behavior, *stop it right now.* Don't put yourself into debt trying to impress people. At the end of the day, you need to secure your financial future. You cannot do this if you are spending beyond your means. Remember – Your self-worth is not defined by the possessions you accumulate.

✓ Read the Bible verse *Galatians 1: 10*, let this scripture serve as a reminder to not you're your life trying to please & impress people.

Principle #18.
Plan for Your Growth & Advancement

Many people mistakenly believe that if they do a good job, upper management will appreciate their value and automatically reward and promote them. This is not always the case. To advance your career, you must be strategic about it. Here's how:

1. Map out your career goals on paper. Where do you want to be professionally two years from now? Five years from now? Seven to ten years from now? What steps do you need to take to get to the next level? Is there one goal that will accelerate all of the other goals? Write it down in clear, measurable terms. Set deadlines. The subconscious mind responds to dates and deadlines.
2. Identify the three most important attributes that you need to advance to the next two levels. Don't just develop the skills and traits to land your supervisor's job, think about what you need to do to become your supervisor's supervisor. Figure out where you measure up. Then, develop a game plan to close the gap between where you are now and where you want to be in two to five years.
3. Brian Tracy, who is a well know peak performance consultant & author talks about a concept called Zero Based Thinking, which is, knowing what you now know is there anything that you're doing today that you

wouldn't get involved in again? Any commitment of time and resources that you would not repeat again? Any job or field that you're working in that is preventing you from increasing your value and earning potential? If the answer is yes, then the next question is how quickly can you get out and how fast?

4. Gain a better understanding of what your CEO and board expect and respect. Then become the kind of person that they can groom for advancement.

5. Identify your immediate and ultimate career goals. Write down the next three steps that you'll take beginning this week, to move closer to your goals.

6. Cultivate more effective and mutually beneficial relationships. Think about your goals and build strategic alliances with people who can help you get there.

7. Seek out evaluations from your supervisor, mentor or a professional coach. Ask them to identify: your strengths, areas for growth, skills you need to learn and experiences that you need to seek out in order to move closer to your goals.

8. Be an original, but make sure you also know how to align with your organization's values and culture.

9. Volunteer for assignments that provide high visibility and additional responsibility.

10. Constantly look for ways to challenge yourself. Seek out new opportunities and challenges to help you hone your skills.

11. Keep a log of the various ways that you've added value to the organization. If you can track how your efforts and ideas have led to increased productivity and revenue or reduced costs, you are showing your boss that you are an asset to the organization.
12. Become familiar and conversant in the subjects that are of the utmost importance to manager's two levels higher than you.
13. Turn your car or subway ride into a mini learning center by listening to professional development and personal enrichment audio programs.
14. Don't wait for your supervisor to send you to a training program. Take the initiative and seek out training programs that pique your interest and are relevant to your job function.
15. Meet with a top manager in your organization and volunteer to do an assignment for them that does not conflict with your current job function or your supervisor's objectives for you.
16. Seek out a mentor. Find someone who is further along in their career and schedule regular meetings about once a month to discuss questions, concerns and strategic career moves.
17. Take responsibility for your career. Do not leave your career in someone else's hands. It's your professional future, take charge of it.

Questions for You To Give Some Thought To

Following are some questions designed to get you thinking about ways to plan for your growth and advancement.

- Where do you see yourself professionally one year from now? What about five years from now? What's your plan to get there?
- What is the one thing that you can do today to put your career plan into motion?

Action Steps

✓ Take a few minutes and identify the position you would like to have in five years. Be specific. Then, review your resume and make sure that the skills, tasks and experiences listed on your resume reflect the type of position you're aiming for.

✓ If you are planning to stay with your current company, get a copy of your company's organizational chart. Circle the position or positions that you are aspiring to. Then, learn everything you need to learn so you can apply for that position or something similar.

✓ Select one of the career advancement tips that I laid out for you & get started on one this week.

✓ Read the Bible verse *Proverbs 21: 5*, let this scripture serve as a reminder to diligently plan your desired career path.

Principle #19.
Turn Your Car or Subway Ride Into A Traveling University

Sometimes when your plate is full and you're juggling multiple priorities it can be difficult to find time for personal development. I get it. But when you carve out time to invest in yourself you become a more self-actualized human and you position yourself for better opportunities. If you are short on time like most people, one of the best ways to make time for personal development is to turn your car, subway or bus ride into a traveling university. Use your travel time to read books and listen to personal growth and professional development audio programs.

It is well documented that the average person reads about one book a year and spends less than 10% of their time developing themselves. If you commit to reading one book per month and spend your travel time reading and listening to personal development programs, you'll be way ahead of the game. This puts you in the driver's seat of your career and your life.

The simple fact is people who know more have a greater advantage over people who don't. They have more opportunities available to them, a wider & more diverse network, they can move comfortably in diverse social circles without feeling out of place and they tend to advance more quickly in their careers. Also, other people tend to gravitate toward individuals who know more because they respect their opinion and expertise. Being knowledgeable has nothing to do with social status or formal education. It's about being well read and versed in a variety of topics. You can do this by spending time developing yourself.

Routinely look for ways to expand your skills and knowledge. You'll not only grow personally, but financially and professionally as well. Become a student of life.

Questions for You To Give Some Thought To

Following are some questions designed to get you thinking about ways to invest in your personal development.

- What topics would you like to learn more about? Pick one & start investing in your learning.
- How much television do you watch each day? How much time do you spend on social media? How much more could you learn if you cut back on the amount of television & social media that you consume each day?
- Are there any skills that if fine-tuned would help you get ahead in your industry? What kinds of books should you be reading to help you grow as a person and advance your career?

Action Steps

✓ Leaders are readers. Commit to reading one book per month. Even if it's an audio book.
✓ Establish a rule of cutting back on television unless you are watching a discovery, biography, business or personal growth program.
✓ Be teachable. In order to learn, you've got to be teachable. If you are a know-it-all, you will continually close your mind to new ideas, new information and new perspectives thus stunting your growth.
✓ Read the Bible verse *Proverbs 12: 1*, let this scripture serve as a reminder that discipline and knowledge go hand-in-hand.

Principle # 20.
Get Ready

Have you ever heard the saying: *"Luck happens when preparation meets opportunity?"* With this in mind: If your big break were to come, would you be ready? I'm talking about totally ready – in mind, attitude and habits.

This is an important question to ask, because many well-meaning people with good intentions blew great opportunities because they were not ready. Talking like you are ready is not the same as being ready. Looking the part gets you closer, but it still is not the same as being ready. To get ready, you must position yourself by fine-tuning and pruning the areas in your life that need to be fine-tuned and pruned. This way you'll be prepared mentally, emotionally and behaviorally to recognize and act on opportunities cleverly disguised as change, coincidence or challenges.

Whatever you need to do to get ready, start now by identifying 5 to 10 things that you can do to put yourself in a better position to achieve the things in life that you want to achieve. Do you need to go back to school? Learn something new? Become more computer savvy? Gain some hands-on experience? Resolve some longstanding issues? Break away from certain people? Do more networking?

Don't waste any more time. Start doing what you need to do to get ready. This way when your big break comes, you'll be 100% ready for it.

Questions for You To Give Some Thought To

Following are some questions designed to get you thinking about ways to get ready.

- Where can it be said that you need to get ready? What are you going to do about it?
- Are you putting in the work to get ready? What is your evidence of this?

Action Steps

✓ Take up a new hobby. Learn everything there is to learn about it.
✓ Be professional in all that you do – professional in dress, speech, writing and demeanor.
✓ Rather than shying away from something challenging or difficult, keep the end-goal in mind and push yourself to stretch yourself.
✓ Read the Bible verse *Proverbs 24: 27*, let this scripture serve as a reminder of the importance of being prepared.

Principle #21.
Use Failure As A Gauge for Growth

A big part of success is in knowing that failure comes with the journey. The only way to avoid failure is to never leave your house. Even then if you stay home long enough you will probably fail at something. So, the issue here is not whether you are going to fail. It's whether you are going to fail forward – meaning that you allow yourself to learn from your setbacks so that you can use your experiences to take your life to the next level. Always remember that the difference between a successful person and an unsuccessful one is how they view and handle failure.

Successful people do not allow themselves to become defeated by failure even when they are temporarily knocked off their feet. Instead, they use failure to their advantage by forecasting into the future and thinking about how they can improve their odds next time around. In essence, they use failure as a mileage marker to measure how far they've come, how much further they need to go and what they need to do differently going forward.

Always remember that you cannot have success without failure. Failure is an essential part of the success journey because it expands your vantage point and teaches you what not to do next time around. Believe it or not, every time you fail you get one step closer to your ultimate goal. Because, you now have the life experience to foresee potential problems and discern situations that are likely to knock you off course. While information provides you with knowledge, failure and introspection provide you with wisdom.

Failure also has another benefit: It makes you more resourceful. When you turn your setbacks into your steps to success, you strengthen your internal resolve. As a result, you develop the resilience to reevaluate your plans and redirect your efforts so that you can make your life work no matter what happens to you along the way.

Remember failure does not necessarily mean that you are on the wrong path. It simply means that you may have to take a different route or make some adjustments along the way. When you fall, get back up and get back in the game. Whenever you experience a setback, make the decision to turn your setbacks into your steps to success.

Questions for You To Give Some Thought To

Following are some questions designed to get you thinking about how you are going to handle failure.

- What lessons have you learned from failure?
- How can you turn your setbacks into success?

- Who else has experienced this same challenge and how did they handle it?
- Knowing what you now know what will you do differently next time around?

Action Steps

✓ Use failure as a gauge for growth. Instead of internalizing failure and beating up on yourself, build failure into your success plan. Use failure to gauge the skills that you need to develop in order to grow.
✓ Build failure into the big picture of your overall life plan. All successful companies have something called a contingency plan built into their strategic plan. A contingency plan is a plan specifically designed to deal with setbacks, crisis and unwanted situations that are likely to occur. Take a page from the books of the big companies by learning to build failure into the big picture of your life plan. This way, when setbacks happen instead of caving under pressure you'll be able to bounce back more readily.
✓ Resolve to never give up.
✓ Read the Bible verse *James 1: 5*, let this scripture serve as a reminder that you whenever you fail or fall, you can go to the scriptures for wisdom and you can pray for wisdom.

Principle #22.
When You're Going Through Hell, Don't Stop To Take Pictures

When you're going through tough times it's perfectly natural to vent about it. It's also natural to feel a little discouraged when life seems like its frowning on you. But at some point, after you've given yourself enough time to recover, you've got to make the decision to rise above the setback or maneuver around it.

Wallowing in your pain does nothing to move your life forward. All it does is keep you stuck. Each and every one of us encounters setbacks. The key is learning how to bounce back and keep on keeping on.

There's a saying that goes, *"When you're going through hell don't stop to take pictures."* Implicit in this statement is when you are going through a tough time don't stay in your pain indefinitely. Stop talking about how bad and sad you feel all the time. Stop saying that you will never recover from the setback. Instead, resolve to keep on keeping on, no matter what. Yes, this is easier said than done, but it is not impossible. When life knocks you down, don't stay down. Make the decision to get up and never let up, even if you feel sad and scared in the process.

Have you ever watched a toddler learning to walk? What happens? They take a few steps and fall. Sometimes they bump into things. Sometimes they hit their heads and stub their toes. And sometimes they collapse or completely fall on their bottoms. But no matter how many times they fall down, bump their heads or have unforeseen objects tumble down on them, they keep getting back up....and eventually they learn to walk.

As adults we tend to forget that like the toddler when we fall down we have the ability to get back up. As a result, when we encounter hard times or feel like we've come to the end of our rope we allow difficult circumstances and feelings of hopelessness to keep us down.

There is no circumstance around you more powerful than the power that lies within you. When life knocks you down, you must call upon your toddler powers – your powers of determination, perseverance and sheer will power so that you can steady yourself and get back up.

It is this will to try and try again that enables you to keep moving even when the odds are stacked against you. And the longer you persist, the more determined you will become to rise. So when life knocks you down, be like a toddler and get back up.

Questions for You To Give Some Thought To

Following are some questions designed to get you thinking about how you are going to develop the resolve to keep pressing on.

- Often when we go through an extremely trying experience we ask: *Why me?* But asking this question does little to help you move forward. It keeps you stuck, tied to the pain of the experience, a perpetual victim with no help in sight. A more empowering question is: *What now?* With this in mind: *What now? Where are you going to go from here?*

- Recall a difficult experience that you thought would knock the wind out of your sails but somehow you survived it. Looking back, what have you learned about yourself, particularly concerning your resilience, courage and resourcefulness?

Action Steps

✓ Gain is almost always disguised as loss like: the job you lost that opened the door to a better one, the partner who left or mistreated you but opened the door for someone better to come along. What losses in your life were actual gains, now that you've had some time to look back and reflect? Write them down to remind you that a loss in one area is usually a gain in another.

✓ New Story Exercise: Where might you be right now if your difficult experience did not happen to you? Write a page of this fantasy. Let your thoughts have fun with this exercise. Now come back to reality and remind yourself that every end is a new beginning. Re-write your story honoring where you are now and how you will use your experiences for the next chapter of your life.

✓ <u>Back In Time Exercise</u>: Pretend that you could go back in time and undue one of your most painful experiences. If you knew then what you know now, what would you do differently? Since you cannot go back in time, think of all the ways that you can apply the lessons learned through painful life experiences to other facets of your life. What's the resounding message that you hear? Make this message, your mantra.

✓ Read the Bible verse *Romans 8: 28* let this scripture serve as a reminder that all things can be worked out for your good and your growth.

Principle #23.
Sometimes You've Got To Trip Your Way Into Walking

Rashad was four months out of recovery. To the casual observer he looked like any other addict hooked on drugs. But there was something different going on inside of him. He was beginning to see inklings of his greatness. This time, he was determined to stay clean and gain his life back. But, since this was Rashad's third time recovering from a relapse, nobody believed him and nobody trusted that he was finally through with the drugs this time. As far as Rashad's friends and family were concerned, he was talking a good game, but the proof remained to be seen.

This did not discourage Rashad one bit. He was a man on a mission. A mission to get his life back. So even if no one else believed him, he knew that he could not afford to not believe in himself. Rashad may have made some poor choices in the past, but if he knew nothing else, he knew that he was tired of living beneath his potential. He also knew that this time he was finally done with the drugs. Rashad may have fallen down a few times, but this time he was determined to get back up.

My grandmother used to say: *Sometimes you've got to trip your way into walking.* In life, there are some people who learn their lessons the first time around and others who've got to repeat the lesson over and over again until they stop doing the things that cause them pain and drama. Taking longer to arrive at your destination does not mean that you can't or won't get there. It simply means that for whatever reason you've got some additional twists and turns to take before you can get to your place of destiny. Perhaps there were important signposts that you missed or cautionary lights that you ignored. Maybe you were speeding and put yourself in red light situations when you should have slowed down and stayed in the green zone. Regardless of where you are in your life's journey, here's what you must remember, no matter how many times you fall, you have what it takes to get back up.

There's a song by Donnie McClurkin entitled, "We Fall Down." In the song he sings about how a saint is just a sinner who fell and got up. He sings about how there is a seed of righteousness in all of us that cannot stay down. Whenever I hear this song, I am reminded of the awesome power of God who can restore us to our original place of righteousness no matter hard we fall, how low we go, how many people stop believing in us and how many promises we've made and broken.

Today, no matter how far you've fallen, claim your seed of righteousness and get back up. And if you happen to trip and fall along the way, claim your seed of righteousness and get back up again and again and again and again...

Questions for You To Give Some Thought To

Following are some questions designed to help you find your way back to you.

- Who do you know that has fallen down, but got back up? What lessons can you take from their life?
- Sometimes we fall down because we don't pay attention to the cautionary lights of life that warn us of potential trouble. Looking back, were there any cautionary lights that you ignored? Knowing what you now know, how can you use this experience to grow forward?
- Sometimes when we are in a valley, we become embarrassed about our situation and neglect to reach out for help. But the thing about falling into a valley is there's no place left to go but up. With this in mind, who can you reach out to, to help you get back up?

Action Steps

✓ Sometimes we need the help of others to get back up. Go through your phone and pick someone to talk to. If you don't get the help you need pick someone else. Just keep talking until you find someone who can help you or point you in the right direction.

✓ Read the Bible verse *Proverbs 24:16*, let this scripture serve as a reminder that no matter how far you fall, you have the power to get back up.

Principle # 24.
No Matter How Long The Summer Lasts Winter Always Comes

We've all heard the saying: *To everything there is a season.* There's a time to laugh, a time to cry, a time to live and a time to die, a time for play and a time to rest, a time to plant and a time to harvest. But sometimes when things are good and we get into a comfort zone, we forget that life is seasonal. As a result, we treat life like a never-ending summer vacation and fail to plan for the winter seasons of life.

If you understand the natural ebb and flow of life, you should also understand that no matter how long the summer lasts winter always comes. Have you prepared yourself? Have you put some serious thought into what you are going to do when the well runs dry, the world gets a little colder, money becomes tighter and life changes on you without warning or notice? It's critical that you make provisions for the winter seasons of life because ready or not winter always comes.

Sometimes the winter seasons of life come in the form of: sudden illness, death, the loss of a job, unexpected expenses, the loss of your youth and vitality. There is no way around the natural ebb and flow of life, because as long as you are alive it's going to rain on you from time to time, even if you have an umbrella. However, if you hold on to the notion that everything in life is seasonal, meaning it is subject to change. Then, you can prepare yourself for the winter seasons of life by accepting that, *Shift Happens.*

It's not always easy or pleasant to ride out the winter seasons of life, but if you are to survive in this world, you must learn to adapt when unexpected change comes your way. It is when we truly understand that nothing in life is guaranteed, except death, that we can take comfort in the expression: *And this too shall pass.* If you understand that storms come to pass and not to stay, you can rest in the understanding that somehow, someway, you will get through the trials of life even if it rocks your world in the process.

Questions for You To Give Some Thought To

Following are some questions designed to help you prepare for the winter seasons of life.

- What mental, emotional, spiritual and financial preparations have you made for the winter seasons of life? If you haven't started making provisions yet, when are you going to start?
- If you are not sure where to start, sometimes it's helpful to think back to past winter seasons and how you survived them or how others have survived tough times. With this in mind, what tools have you relied on in the past to help you get through the storms of life? Which of these tools can you put away

now to help you ride out the winter seasons of life?

Action Steps

✓ If you are going through a winter season right now and you feel overwhelmed by it, it is helpful to take inventory of your resources in order to figure out how to best handle the situation. With this in mind, make a list of your resources, (Ex. family, friends, people you can talk to who've been where you are now, cash reserves, ideas to stretch your income, a place to fellowship, your faith and so on.

✓ Often our biggest lessons come from adversity. Ask yourself: Is there anything that life might be trying to teach me through this experience?

✓ Sometimes when you are going through a tough time in your own life, the only way to take your mind off of your situation is to help someone else who is worse off than you. With this in mind, identify one thing that you can do to help someone else who is worse off than you.

✓ Read the Bible verse *Proverbs 6:6 - 11*, let this scripture serve as a reminder that if ants can develop a system to plan for the winter, you can too.

Principle #25
Let Go Of Habits That Do Not Serve You Well

If you engage in a behavior long enough, it eventually becomes a habit. The thing about habits is because they are second-nature to us, we do them without thinking about them. And whenever we are not thinking about what we are doing, we cannot not see how a particular behavior or choice negatively affects our lives. This is why it's critical to pay attention to your habits, especially the ones that do not serve you well.

Are your habits serving you well? If not, it might be well worth the effort to make a few changes. Start by taking an inventory of your habits. Identify the ones that are undesirable or counterproductive. Develop the willpower to eliminate them from your life.

Bad habits can be your worst enemy, especially when they get in the way of your health, happiness and peace of mind. Almost everything you do is a result of your habits, from your morning routine, to what you eat, to the way you wear your hair, to what you do with your leisure time.

The most powerful way to rid yourself of a bad habit is to adopt new behaviors that are more in line with how you want to feel and where you want to end up in life. If you really set your mind to it and adopt the attitude that nothing will stand in your way, you can cast aside any habits that are not consistent with the type of person you want to become.

Questions for You To Give Some Thought To

Following are some questions designed to help you identify any habits that may not be serving you well.

- Are there any bad habits that you've been trying to change, but haven't had much success with? What's stopping you? What's getting in the way of you kicking the habit?

- Discipline is what separates the doers from the excuse makers. Where can it be said that you need to become more disciplined?

Action Steps

✓ Take inventory of your habits. Carefully examine the ones that no longer serve you. Be brutally honest with yourself. Then, make a decision to change.

✓ Some bad habits are more obvious than others like: smoking, excessive shopping and overeating. Then there are those habits that are not as easy to recognize because they're so deeply ingrained in our personality and patterns that they become our blind spots like: constantly letting people take advantage of you then getting upset because you feel like you've been used, allowing fear to hold you back or continually picking relationship partners who are no good for you. Take a little time to give some serious thought to the less obvious habits that might be holding you back.

✓ If bad habits were easy to break, none of us would have them. Since you already know how difficult it is to change longstanding behaviors, enlist the support of your family and friends.

✓ Read the Bible verse _1 Thessalonians 5: 21_, let this scripture serve as a reminder to hold on to what is good.

Principle #26.
Strive for Balance

Far too many men and women pursue money, status and career advancement at the expense of their happiness and health. To be truly successful you've got to find a way to maintain balance between work and your personal life.

The reason why so many people feel stressed and pressured even though they make a good salary and have achieved many of their goals is that they have no work/life balance. They're all work and no play.

Speaking for myself, as an extremely busy woman who is running a business and a ministry while balancing the demands of motherhood, it would be easy for me to buy into the notion that I have to neglect my own personal life in order to achieve my goals. But this is simply not true because there are too many examples of men and women with successful careers who are balancing competing priorities while maintaining a life outside of work.

Make no mistake about it, without question striking a balance between work and your personal life is a never-ending juggling act. But at the same time the important lesson to keep in mind is: *You cannot neglect what matters most and gain true success.*

To keep things balanced, every month I plan my schedule of speaking engagements, workshops, coaching sessions, business meetings and other tasks related to both the business and ministry. During this time, I also carve out time to review my goals, market the business, and plan the projects that I am working on. However, before I set any calendar dates in stone, I block out time for the things I do in my personal life like: family time, going to museums and other things that I enjoy or that are important to me. Additionally, I block out time to catch up with friends. Naturally, there are times when I must adjust my schedule to accommodate something unexpected, but the goal is balance not running myself into the ground so that my life is not so career-driven that it becomes one-dimensional.

The lesson here is: If you focus solely on acquiring money, you'll come to the end of your life only to realize that the pursuit of success was all for naught. Like the famous line in the movie *Mahogany* says: *Success means nothing without someone you love to share it with.* Don't come to the end of your journey only to realize that your pursuit of success was all for naught.

Questions for You To Give Some Thought To

Following are some questions designed to get you thinking about how you are going to maintain balance.

• Where can it be said that you need to be more balanced?

- Are you putting all of your efforts into one area of your life at the detriment of another? If the answer is yes, what are you going to do to change this?

Action Steps

✓ Carve out time for yourself each day. Better yet, highlight it in your planner.
✓ Imagine that today was your 75th birthday and your younger self came to your older, wiser self for advice about how to live a more balanced life. With this idea in mind, let your older, wiser self write a wisdom letter to the current you advising you on how to achieve greater balance.
✓ Mail the letter to yourself in one week. When you receive it, apply the advice and make a commitment to strive for balance.
✓ Read the Bible verse *Mark 6: 31*, let this scripture serve as a reminder of the importance of rest and balance.

Principle #27.
Make Good Health A Top Priority

Believe it or not, your health is your primary source of wealth, because if you do not have the energy and stamina to pursue your dreams you will not be able to create the life you want. Most of the major causes of premature death are preventable if you are proactive about making your health a top priority. There are hundreds of resources on health and fitness. Your job is to do a little legwork to find what works for you.

Start your healthy lifestyle journey by making the commitment to exercise and eat a balanced diet. Eat more fruits, vegetables and whole grain products. Drink plenty of water. Try to eliminate or at least minimize the amount of carbonated and caffeinated beverages that you drink.

Develop the habit of viewing your body as the temple that houses your plans and dreams or a high-powered machine that requires good fuel to make it through each day with enthusiasm and vigor. Also develop the habit of moving your body daily. This keeps your muscles and joints flexible and agile. Discipline yourself to go to the gym, workout at home, take a dance or martial arts class or take up a sport. Most people hate to exercise, myself included, but when you begin to see the results you'll feel a sense of accomplishment. Plus you'll feel more energized.

In addition to eating well and regular exercise, it is also important that you get enough rest. Early to bed and early to rise makes for a well rested you. Try not to watch television right before bed. Instead, put on some soothing music or curl up with a good book. Wake up one hour earlier each day. Take that hour to invest in yourself. Read, reflect, meditate, pray, exercise and plan your day. Waking up an hour earlier allows you to take time for you without the added pressure of worrying about how you are going to get out on time and make it through the daily rush. This enables you to experience a sense of calm as you begin each day.

Make peace of mind a personal priority. Learn to choose your battles. Stay away from people who are prone to drama or who bring constant discord to your life. Your peace of mind is an important part of your health...your mental health.

Last but not least, get regular medical and dental check-ups. With all of the advances we have in the medical field, if you have any health issues getting a regular check-up allows you to catch any health concerns early.

Questions for You To Give Some Thought To

Following are some questions designed to get you thinking about ways to make your health more of a priority.

- How would regular exercise and a well balanced diet enhance your life?

- What foods should you be eating more of? What should you be eating less of?
- Are you drinking enough water? Are you getting enough rest?

Action Steps

✓ Write out a detailed description of your ideal health and wellness state. What would you look like? How would you feel? What would you have the energy to do or try?

✓ Set clear health and fitness goals for yourself. Set goals for your weight and your mental well-being.

✓ Figure out which health habits you need to take on right now that can serve as a springboard for your new health and fitness lifestyle.

✓ Read the Bible verse *1 Corinthians 6: 19-20*, let this scripture serve as a reminder that your body is your temple so take care of it.

Principle #28
Get Out Of Your Comfort Zone

If you want to achieve radical results you've got to do something that you've never done before – something that stretches you, forces you to grow, upgrades your skills, unlocks your potential and challenges you to rise to higher heights of excellence. And whatever you do, do not allow fear to hold you back.

Far too often, fear is the only thing that stands in the way of you and your dreams. Believe it or not, we come into this world with only two fears: the fear of falling and the fear of loud noises. All other fears are learned responses.

Fear is one of the most dangerous time bandits. Why? Because fear discourages you from pursuing your dreams, trying new things and it causes you to stay in situations that you have outgrown. Whenever you feel fearful of trying something new or difficult, remind yourself that you have what it takes to make it. If that doesn't work feel the fear and do it anyway. What have you got to lose? Today, take the plunge and get out of your comfort zone.

Questions for You To Give Some Thought To

Following are some questions designed to get you thinking about ways to get out of your comfort zone.

- It takes great courage to get out of your comfort zone. But I'll bet that you act courageously all the time. Sometimes courage comes in small doses like: setting boundaries with overbearing people or advocating for those who cannot advocate for themselves. What small acts of courage have enabled you to get out of your comfort zone?

- We always pay for staying in our comfort zone. We pay with unrealized dreams, silent longings and living a life of quiet desperation. One of the worst things that we can do to ourselves is become prisoners of regret. Because regret causes us to look back on our lives from a place of disappointment. Don't allow yourself to live this way. Instead, live courageously. What courageous thing can you do for yourself right now so that you won't have any regrets when you look back over your life?

Action Steps

✓ If you are like most people, I'll bet that there's a long-buried dream or secret wish that still lurks in the back of your mind. If so, why not explore a little and see where your dream takes you. Stop telling yourself that it's too late, you're too old, you've got too many responsibilities or that you don't have what it takes to do it. Be brave enough to look your dream right in the eye and go for it.

✓ Sometimes you've got to make a few adjustments in your dream in order to make allowances for the new factors operating in your life. If this is the case, make the alterations you need to make. Then go out and make your dream come true. No excuses. No regrets.

✓ Read the Bible verse *2 Timothy 1: 7*, let this scripture serve as a reminder that you don't have to stay stuck in fear.

Principle #29.
Get Intentional About Your Happiness

How happy are you right now? Do you even know? Perhaps you think you'll be happier when you get a bigger house, a higher paying job, lose the extra weight or find someone wonderful to share your life with.

Most people, myself included, treat happiness like a prize we win for achieving our goals or a euphoric feeling that comes from something outside of ourselves. But true happiness is a state of mind, one that we can consciously choose by becoming more aware of the little things in life that put a smile on our face and make us feel contented on the inside.

The reason so many of us believe that happiness comes from something external is we've become brainwashed by a culture that glorifies excess and materialism. It's easy to lose sight of what really matters, when we are constantly bombarded with images that tell us we need something outside of ourselves to become happy and whole. But if we are to live happy and fulfilled lives, we've got to realize that happiness does not come from the things that we acquire or the circumstances in our lives, it comes from choosing to live with a sense of joy each day and appreciating the little things in life.

Happiness is not a feeling. It is a choice. It took me a long time to realize this, because for most of my life I allowed my moods and circumstances to dictate my outlook on life.

The truth is you can be as happy as you choose to be, because a big portion of your happiness is determined by your habitual thoughts, feelings, words and actions. Let me be clear here: You cannot decide to be happy by sitting back and waiting for your life to magically feel joyful by means of osmosis. You have to consciously create a happy state of mind as part of your overall lifestyle, just as you would an exercise regimen. All of your habitual thoughts, feelings, words and actions must be directed toward creating a joyful, appreciative, peaceful and abundant life.

Today, ask yourself: What do I need to be truly happy? Spend some time thinking about this question. Be reflective and contemplative as you uncover the answer. Trust that the answer to this question lies inside of you and that authentic happiness is within your grasp.

Questions for You To Give Some Thought To

Following are some questions designed to get you thinking about how you can make happiness a habit.

- Do you believe that happiness is within your grasp? If not, what will it take for you to be happy?
- Are your thoughts, feelings, words and actions moving you in the direction of

happiness? If not, what are you going to do change this?

- Often, the reason we are unhappy is because we look for happiness to happen to us instead of taking control of our levels of happiness and joy. When was the last time you were truly happy? Looking back now, was it based on something external or something internal? What simple things can you do to increase your level of happiness?

- How many peaceful interludes do you take for yourself each day in order to get in touch with the things that make you happy? If you do not take peaceful interludes, when are you going to start?

Action Steps

✓ Write down a detailed description of what your life would look like if you were just a little bit happier. Use this description to help you figure out what you need to be doing more of to become just a little bit happier.
✓ Develop an attitude of gratitude for everything that is good in your life.
✓ Look at every aspect of your life from a fresh perspective and think about what you can do to bring more joy to each area.
✓ Read the Bible verse *Philippians 4: 11 - 13*, let this scripture teach you the secret to being content in all things.

Principle #30.
Recognize That Your Days Are Numbered

We've all heard the saying: *live each day as if it were your last*. However, most of us treat our lives as if we had an infinite amount of time. We move through life as if we will receive advance notice of when our time is up. We put off so much, delay so many dreams and waste far too many years on people and things that don't really matter.

When you treat each day as if it were your last, the past no longer holds you captive and you don't stress and obsess over what tomorrow may bring. Most importantly, you don't take the seemingly ordinary things for granted. Instead, you simply cherish each day as a gift.

It's only when we truly understand that our days are numbered, that we start to live more fully and appreciatively. We start to embrace and savor the simple mundane experiences like: sipping a fresh brewed cup of coffee or tea, seeing a garden in full bloom, spending time with loved ones, chatting on the phone with an old friend, a warm relaxing bath, walking in the rain, seeing a first snow fall.

Whenever I start feeling sorry for myself or get stuck in a funk that I just can't seem to pull myself out of, I visit an old cemetery. The stillness of it all reminds me that when it's over, it's over. So my best bet is to pick myself up, pull myself out of my little funk and recognize that everyday above ground is far better than any day below it.

So until it is carved out in stone, you've been blessed with a tremendous gift called life. Honor this gift by living each day as fully as you can.

Questions for You To Give Some Thought To

Following are some questions designed to help you live more appreciatively and fully.

- What are you thankful for? How do you convey your gratitude?
- What simple things do you most enjoy?

Action Steps

✓ Imagine that today was your 80th birthday and your younger self came to your older, wiser self for advice about how to live more fully and appreciatively. What would you say? With this idea in mind, let your older, wiser self write a wisdom letter to your current self advising you how to live more fully and appreciatively.

✓ Mail the letter to yourself in one week. When you receive it, apply the advice and make a commitment to live each day more fully.

✓ Read the Bible verse *Ecclesiastes 3: 1*, let this scripture serve as a reminder to cherish and respect your gift of time.

Principle #31.
Learn To Forgive, Not For Them
...For You

One of life's greatest teaching tools was giving us the power to remember the past without the power to go back and change it. This provides us with an authentic opportunity for spiritual growth. The power to remember the past without the ability to change it seems like a double-edged sword especially when it comes to the issue of forgiveness.

Forgiving someone who has hurt you is not always easy. And sometimes it's even harder to forgive the ones you love, because often the expectation is: If they love you then they will not hurt you. But people are not perfect. People will mess up...big time, including the people you love.

What many people who chose to remain resentful fail to realize is when you refuse to forgive, you become a prisoner of your own bitterness. How does this happen? Because when you are consumed with resentment it eventually seeps into the other areas of your life. Even more, while the person who has wronged you has moved on and is not even thinking about you, you are allowing that person to have an effect on you.

Forgiveness is not something that you do for the other person; it is something that you do for yourself. The longer you hold on to negative feelings the more you become consumed by them. This prevents you from fully enjoying your life.

This is why it is so important to forgive. Some people confuse forgiveness with being a doormat or allowing people to get away with mistreating you. This is not forgiveness. You can forgive someone and still want to see justice (not revenge). You can forgive someone and still choose not to have a relationship with them, especially if the person is toxic.

Forgiveness does not necessarily mean reconciliation. You may never see the person again but you can still choose to forgive them in your heart by letting go of the hate.

So what does forgiveness look like? Here are three steps that will help you on your forgiveness journey.

1. Give Up the Desire to Get Even

After someone has hurt or betrayed us, the natural inclination is to want to get even. We want the other person to feel our pain, get a taste of their own medicine. But the problem with having a tit-for-tat attitude is you can never truly get even. You can cause pain, devastation and destruction but you cannot get even. What's done is done. It's fine to want justice. It's perfectly reasonable to fight for it. But there's a fine line between seeking justice and plotting revenge.

2. Try Not to Allow Negative Feelings to Eat Away At You.

It's perfectly healthy to be angry with someone who has offended you, but it's very unhealthy to allow negative feelings to eat away at you. There comes a time when you have to release the negative feelings that you are holding on to. Otherwise you will never move on. Holding on to bitterness is like swallowing a bottle of poison and expecting the other person to become sick by it. It simply doesn't work that way.

3. Understand That Forgiveness Is A Commitment To The Process of Letting Go

When you view forgiveness as a commitment to the process of letting go of the pain and resentment that is eating away at you instead of seeing it as letting the offending party get away with hurting you or taking something away from you, you begin to feel more in control of your life. You also empower yourself by consciously shifting your focus from being a victim to living victoriously. While forgiveness may not happen overnight, if you are committed to the process of letting go, you will come to find that it is certainly an attainable state. It may even take years depending on the circumstances, but if you make a conscious effort not to allow bitterness to get the best of you, you will find emotional freedom because you will no longer define your life by past hurts or slights.

Questions for You To Give Some Thought To

Following are some questions designed to get you thinking about how to begin the process of forgiveness.

- Think about a person who you have forgiven who you thought you would never be able to forgive. How can you call upon these same internal tools to forgive the person or people whom you need to forgive now?

- Few things are ever just black and white. Most situations contain shades of gray. Are there any gray areas that you may have overlooked? How can you use the gray areas as a starting point for forgiveness?

Action Steps

✓ You can turn all hurtful experiences into tools for empowerment by using forgiveness as the foundation. Always remember that no matter what happens to you, you have two choices: You can choose to become a prisoner of resentment or you can choose to take steps to move forward.

✓ Read the Bible verse *Luke 6: 37*, let this scripture serve as a reminder of the importance of forgiveness.

Principle #32.
Tap Into The Power of Prayer

There are many personal benefits to prayer. Prayer focuses the mind, strengthens the spirit, calms emotions and increases your ability to access your internal wisdom and discern different situations. Prayer empowers us to take action on behalf of our neighbors all around the world who are struggling and suffering. Prayer reduces the ego. It teaches us humility and patience. Prayer enables us to release painful emotions and forgive others for their transgressions. It deepens our relationships and connection to God. Prayer has in it a great dynamic force that fortifies us to face life with inner resolve and spiritual strength.

There are many ways to tap into the power of prayer. You can pray alone or with other people. You can pray at home, outdoors or at your place of worship. Prayer can be spoken or offered in the form of a poem, dance or song. Payer can consist of a series of thoughts inside your head as you still your mind. Sometimes there are no words spoken at all. Instead it's more of a contemplative period of thought where you are spending meditative time with an increased awareness of God's presence.

Never underestimate the power of prayer, especially as it relates to your success journey. Prayer is the one of most powerful tools that you have at your disposal. When you feel uncertain about a situation, apprehensive about something or you simply need more clarity before making a decision; pray on it. When life feels overwhelming and you begin to doubt your ability to live the life that you desire the smartest thing that you can do is pray for direction and clarity. Prayer really does change things. If it doesn't change the situation, it will change your outlook about it and give you the resolve to get through it. Tap into the power of prayer and uncover the many wonderful benefits that await you.

Questions for You To Give Some Thought To

Following are some questions designed to get you thinking about ways that you can tap into the power of prayer.

- Men and women who are both successful and spiritually evolved understand the awesome benefits of prayer. What can you do to incorporate prayer as part of your daily routine and success strategy?
- Being spiritually connected involves prayer and meditation. What can you do to become more present in the moment, more aware of yourself, your blessings and God's presence?
- Read the Bible verse *Mark 6: 31*, let this scripture serve as a reminder of the importance of rest and balance.

Action Steps

✓ A big part of becoming more spiritually centered involves shifting your outlook from living life through the lens of an external focus to an internal one. The Creator has given each of us a wonderful tool called intuition that if utilized correctly can serve as a guide. Spend some time this week sharpening your spiritual antenna. Pay closer attention to how you feel around different people and different situations. Trust your intuition more.

✓ Sometimes, in order to get in tune with the divine, you've got to tune some things out. Think of all the ways that you can tune out the noise of the outside world in order to get more in tune with your higher self. As you identify the many ways that you can become more in tune with your higher self, put at least one method into practice.

✓ If you are feeling off balance or out of sorts, get up ½ hour earlier and pray for clarity. Be still and reflective as the answers come to you.

✓ Read the Bible verse _Matthew 7: 7-8_, let this scripture serve as a reminder to ask, seek and knock through prayer.

Principle #33.
Get To The Root of Any Issues That Are Holding You Back Emotionally

There's an old saying that goes: *You can always tell what kind of fruit a tree will bear by looking at the root.* If the root is healthy, then the tree will bear good fruit. But if the root is not healthy then it will produce damaged fruit. What kind of fruit are you producing in your life? This is an important question to ask yourself because if you don't deal with the root of your issues, you will keep yielding results that produce fruitless outcomes.

Every human being on the planet has had bad things happen to them or things that have wounded us emotionally. Some of us have been through traumatic situations that we don't want anyone else to know about. No one is exempt from life's lemons and curveballs. We have all said and done things at some point in our lives that we are not too proud of. Even more, many of us have had things happen to us that were so terribly painful that in order to keep the weight of the trauma from breaking us down, we mentally block it out in an attempt to erase the past.

But here's the irony of life: What doesn't come out in the wash is bound to come out in the rinse. There's no way around it. Because life will do whatever is necessary for us to grow, even if it means forcing us to confront the very issue we think we cannot face. This is how we get to the root of our issues. It is through critical self-examination and getting to the "Why?" behind our thought patterns, actions and choices that undermine our confidence, success and progress.

In order to put your past in its place – which is behind you, you've got to go deeper than the surface to find out why you do the things you do. Some questions you might want to ask yourself are: *Why do I feel this way every time (fill in the blank) happens? Why am I always so defensive? Why do I get bent out of shape so easily? Why am I always angry with so and so? Why do I feel that I must always be right or prove myself? Why do I always feel inadequate? Why will I never let anyone get close to me? Why do I always find a way to sabotage my relationships? What is at the root of my issues?* Only when you get to the root of your issues and start dealing with the source of what's holding you back emotionally can you expect to live a full and empowered life.

While it may be frightening to dig beneath the surface, the truth is if you are to grow to your fullest potential, you've got to look your issues straight in the eye and deal with them.

When you hold on to the issues in your life that create pain, shame and fear, you hold yourself hostage to the pain, shame and fear. This puts a block on your blessings.

Believe it or not, when the painful and shameful things in your life begin to come to the surface, it is life's way of telling you that you are more than capable of handling the issues in your life that you need to address. This enables you to move forcefully into your future.

Whether the root of your issues come from: rejection, abandonment, abuse, neglect, not having your childhood needs met, being unfavorably compared to someone else, or being made to feel like you were a burden, the bottom line is if you don't deal with it now, then it will continue to have a hold on you. Even more, it will seep out into the other facets of your life and hold you back from the fulfilling and rewarding life that you deserve.

Unresolved issues affect every relationship you'll ever have, every goal you'll ever set out to accomplish and every thought that percolates inside your head. Most of our baggage, no matter how small always has roots than run deep. When you get to the root of your issues, you empower yourself to resolve them.

You can be happier, have better relationships and free yourself from the issues that prevent you from being happy and whole, but you have to do your part by addressing them at the root level.

You may have come from a dysfunctional family. You may have come out of an abusive relationship. You may have grown up feeling like an outsider in your own home. Perhaps the people who raised you were unkind, unsupportive, did not accept you or did not love you the way you needed to be loved. And, now you are struggling to pick up the pieces and find your way back to you. Be that as it may, what you must always keep in mind is that no matter what you have gone through in the past, you now have the power to change your life for the better.

The past is the past and you are strong enough to move forward in spite of it. The future is yours for the taking. Your time is now. Seize the moment by making the commitment to heal any excess baggage. Then, watch your life unfold in ways you could not begin to imagine. This is your time. Get to the root of your issues so that you can become a happier, healthier you.

Questions for You To Give Some Thought To

Following are some questions designed to get you thinking about how to get to the root of your issues.

- Are there any issues in your life that you need to address? What are you waiting for?
- What do you think would happen if you looked your issues straight in the eye and put in the work to come to terms with them? How would your life change for the better?

Action Steps

✓ Take out a sheet of paper. Draw a circle. Inside the circle write down the issues in your life that are sabotaging your success or holding you back in any way. It could be a habit, a defense mechanism, a reaction that you know you need to work on. For example, if you know that you have a tendency to keep people at a distance in order to avoid getting hurt, write that down as an issue. Next to each issue, write down how behaving this way has served you and how it has hindered you. *(Ex. Behaving this way has served me by preventing me from getting hurt but it has also hindered me because it has prevented me from building meaningful connections with other people.* Next, write the adjustments that you need to make so that you can begin to address this issue. *(Ex. In order to begin working on this issue I need to slowly let people into my life and give them a fair chance before deciding that I cannot trust them.)* Lastly, write the name of an individual or a helpful resource that you can go to for support with this issue. It could be a local therapist in your community, support group or a place of worship. Outside the circle, place the names of the people you may have to stay away from or put a little distance between in order to focus on the self-work that you're about to do.

✓ Pick one issue to work on first. Then, call the individual or organization that you listed in the inner section of your circle. Get their support with your issue. Place your paper in a folder so you can review it when needed. Add names to the inner and outer circles as needed.

✓ If you notice that you have an issue or problem that keeps recurring, it means you need to go deeper because you haven't yet gotten to the root. Make the commitment to do a critical self-analysis so that you can get to the root of any issues that might be holding you back.

✓ Read the Bible verse *Jeremiah 33: 3*, let this scripture serve as a reminder that you can call on God & ask Him to reveal any inner roadblocks that you may not be aware of that are hindering you from living a whole and healed life.

Principle #34.
Enjoy The Ride

If you want to live your best life it is essential that you remain passionate about life – that you approach life with a sense of passion, appreciation and enthusiasm regardless of how routine your life may feel.

Few of us know how blessed we truly are. We focus too much on what's wrong with our lives rather than appreciating what's good about our lives. Believe it or not, this kind of attitude causes us to become stagnant. Anything in life from our jobs to our relationships can become hum drum if we allow it to by simply going through the motions instead of approaching life with a sense of enthusiasm. The key to staying passionate about life is creating small moments of joy and getting up every day with a sense of positive expectation and enthusiasm.

When you simply go through the motions instead of approaching life with a sense of positive expectation, you dishonor your life and take your blessings for granted. You may not have the perfect job, the perfect house, the perfect spouse or the perfect life, but who does? What's more, you're not perfect and you never will be. None of us are. Life is not perfect but it can be good if you choose to remain passionate about it.

Don't let life seat you with skepticism. Do whatever you have to do to stir up your passions so you can bring a renewed sense of appreciation to your job, your relationships and your life. Life is too short to simply go through the motions. If you remain passionate about life you'll enjoy the ride that much more.

Questions for You To Give Some Thought To

Following are some questions designed to get you thinking about simple ways that you can enjoy the ride.

- Where in your life could it be said that you need to become more passionate? What are you going to do about it?
- What milestones and passages in your life have you not celebrated that need to be celebrated? What are you waiting for?
- We all make inner promises to ourselves, but often we fail to keep these promises because we take ourselves for granted. Or we think that "eventually" we'll get around to it. Perhaps you promised yourself that you would go back to school, take a class, join a book club or find one uninterrupted hour a day to have some quality "me" time. What long overdue promises have you made to yourself? What's stopping you from honoring them? What resources, changes in habit or supports are you going to need in order to honor at least one of your inner promises?
- What dreams and passions lie buried inside of you? Why aren't you pursuing these dreams and passions? What convenient

excuses have you made to yourself to rationalize taking your gifts and talents for granted? How can you incorporate some of your dreams and passions into the life you have now?

Action Steps

✓ Think about a long, overdue promise that you've made to yourself. Pick a day this week to honor that promise.

✓ Sometimes it can be difficult to honor our dreams because we don't know what they are. When this happens go back into your childhood for clues. Recall some of your childhood dreams and see if any still hold a special place in your heart today. If so, then resurrect some of your childhood dreams.

✓ Give yourself permission to re-write your script. This may seem like an easy step, but many of us, myself included have a tough time allowing ourselves to wholeheartedly believe that we are entitled to live life by our own design and not by default. So stand in front of a mirror and declare out loud, *I am giving myself permission to re-write my script.*

✓ Get a journal and write out your story. Start by saying. My name is _____. And from this moment on this is the story of my life..._____.

✓ Read the Bible verse *Psalm 118: 24*, let this scripture serve as a reminder to rejoice each day that you are blessed to see another sunrise.

Principle #35.
Treat People Well

Always remember the golden rule of life: *Treat people the way that you want to be treated.* In essence, treat people well. Most people enter into relationships trying to figure out what other people can do for them instead of looking for opportunities to build mutually beneficial relationships. This is the wrong approach because it sets us up to approach our relationships from a position of selfishness. People who want to live prosperously understand that when you sow into the lives of others, you create a cycle of reciprocity in which other people will sow into your life too.

Be a giver rather than a taker by making relationship deposits wherever you go. When you meet someone who you'd like to connect with, instead of trying to find out: What's solely in it for you? Ask yourself: How can I become a greater blessing to this person who I am trying to get to know better or who I am seeking assistance from?

Be good to people wherever you go because you never know how one little random act of kindness can brighten someone's day. Imagine what the world would be like if everyone decided to treat each other well. Our communities would be safer. Our children would grow up feeling nurtured and encouraged. Our jobs would feel more fulfilling and we would be happier, healthier and more productive citizens.

The other part about treating people well is it enables you to broaden your network. And you never know when you may need to call on some of those relationships. People may not remember your name, where you come from or what you do for a living, but they will always remember how you treated them.

Questions for You To Give Some Thought To

Following are some questions designed to get you thinking about ways that you can treat people well.

- In what ways can you become a more giving person?
- In what ways can you become more intentional about extending kindness?

Action Steps

✓ Make a commitment to treat people well.
✓ Think about one thing that you can do to promote goodwill and pay it forward.
✓ Read the Bible verse *Matthew 7: 12*, let this scripture serve as a reminder to do to others as you would have them do to you.

What To Do Next

After reading this book you now have a system of principles to in place position yourself for greater success and achievement. You now have a clear pathway to put some clear steps in place to accelerate your path to success. You are better equipped to leverage your time and talent to create the life you want. You've asked yourself the right questions. Now I invite you to take the next step and sign up for **private premium coaching**.

Whenever we step into a new season of life, we must develop new tools, skills and strategies to help us get where we want to go. When we have the right knowledge, the right frameworks, the right techniques and the right tools we become empowered to achieve our goals with greater clarity and ease. We are better prepared to step into the journey that we are about to embark on with greater confidence and competence.

The real value of being in a coaching relationship with a life coach who is both bible-based and is a veteran professional development consultant is twofold: First, the Bible is replete with wisdom for life. Second the tips, tools and tactics that Cassandra will teach and coach you in are time-tested, practical and solution-focused.

Whether you want to focus on leadership development, mastering your mindset or emotional management, coaching with

Cassandra Mack will help you get unstuck, create a sustainable plan to help you achieve your desired results and provide you with strategies to move your life in the direction that you want to go in with greater clarity, confidence, and effectiveness.

What makes coaching with Cassandra Mack, exceptionally beneficial is, Cassandra bridges the psychology of success, the dynamics of human behavior, and timeless Biblical principles with her innovative empowerment strategies and 20 plus years of successful experience as an executive coach, master facilitator, social worker and thought leader to help individuals and organization build capacity and facilitate success. As a result, Cassandra Mack offers her clients a deeper understanding of what's driving their behavior, what's hindering their success and how to tap their inner strengths and unrealized potential which in turn enables them to achieve their goals faster utilizing her unique techniques to make their lives better.

➢ Are you ready to live a more inspired, and intentional life? Try a coaching session with Cassandra Mack and start seizing your success and repositioning yourself for victorious living. For more information go to: **StrategiesForEmpoweredLiving.com**

Bring A Cassandra Mack Keynote or Workshop To Your Event or Organization

Are you an HR Director or executive facing organizational or employee challenges that need to be addressed sooner than later? Cassandra Mack has helped hundreds of individuals, nonprofit organizations and government agencies develop effective ways to deal with workplace issues that impact performance and productivity. Executives, HR and Organizational Development directors have used Cassandra Mack to tackle some of the most common challenges that plague work environments, such as: ineffective or toxic communication, low team morale, workplace conflict, lack of productivity, misalignment about roles on a team, leading others towards their best success and how to coach, counsel and mentor employees for maximum productivity.

From leadership development for your executive level managers and supervisory skills for new supervisors to professionalism and personal effectiveness for your entire team; Cassandra Mack can work with your organization to help you achieve your desired results. Whether you want to maximize the diverse gifts and talents of your leaders; equip your front-line staff with the essential skills to align with vision, build team cohesion, communicate better, boost morale or adapt well to new changes, Cassandra Mack can assist you. Cassandra Mack's educational courses and professional development learning programs will help you reach your goals faster and empower your staff to do their jobs with greater skill, ease and effectiveness.

Following are 7 Benefits to bringing a Cassandra Mack Training Program to your organization:

1. Increase the collective knowledge of your entire team towards organizational alignment even when they have vastly different viewpoints and work styles.
2. Help your employees function better interpersonally so that managers spend less time refereeing conflicts and misunderstandings.
3. Cultivate future leaders for your organization. When a manager leaves the company, there is often a decline in productivity due to the company not being able to fill the position with a qualified candidate. But with targeted training, you can help ensure your current workforce is prepared to seamlessly move up the ladder as needed.
4. Enable managers/supervisors to develop a better assessment of their employees' strengths, professional-development needs consequently maximizing employee retention and growth.
5. Better prepare your employees to strengthen the essential workplace soft skills that are needed to make good decisions, problem solve, complete tasks accurately and more.

6. Help your staff to align their conduct, work habits and attitude with the culture, mission and vision of your organization as well as the goals of each department within your company.
7. Make it easier for your organization to know where to plan, budget and allocate learning & development resources by evaluating the outcome of the training.

> ➤ For more information about Cassandra Mack's training courses go to: **StrategiesForEmpoweredLiving.com**

If You Enjoyed This Book Leave A Review On Amazon

If you enjoyed this book or received value from it in any way, then I'd like to ask you for a favor: would you be kind enough to leave a review for this book on Amazon? It'd be greatly appreciated! Your Amazon reviews help to get this book into more hands that need to hear this message. Thank you.

About the Author...Cassandra Mack

Cassandra Mack is a trained social worker, successful author, life skills strategist, corporate trainer, and an ordained minister who started her professional career in the social service sector managing and directing programs for youth and conducting educational workshops and life skills support groups for adults.

In 2000 she left her job as the director of youth services for one of the most dynamic social services organizations in NYC to start her own consulting business as a corporate trainer and master facilitator.

Cassandra's company, *Strategies for Empowered Living Inc.*, is a training and development company that provides training, coaching and consulting to help individuals and organizations maximize potential, build capacity and facilitate success.

Cassandra is the founder of, *Cassandra Mack Ministries,* a ministry that utilizes print and social media to train, mentor and equip people with Kingdom-based empowerment tools for victorious living. Every Sunday she hosts *The Sunday Morning Hour of Power Call,* which is affectionately known as *Church By Phone.* Cassandra speaks at churches, corporations, clubs, and national conferences.

She has written more than ten books that are widely utilized in the human services. Cassandra is the voice of counsel to thousands around the world through her books, seminars, Bible-based teaching calls, Facebook Pages, Youtube videos and coaching programs. For more information visit: **StrategiesForEmpoweredLiving.com**

Other Books By Cassandra Mack

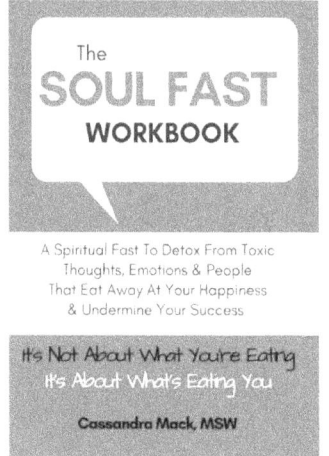

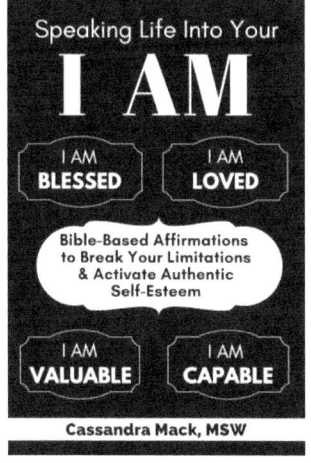

Available at: Amazon.com

www.ingramcontent.com/pod-product-compliance
Lightning Source LLC
Chambersburg PA
CBHW052322220526
45472CB00001B/222

9 781980 417507